Origami per bambini

Young Scholar

**All rights reserved. No part of this document may be reproduced
Used or transmitted in any form or by any means, electronic or otherwise. This means you
cannot photocopy any material ideas or tips that are provided in this book.**

Young Scholar
An imprint of Ciparum LLC

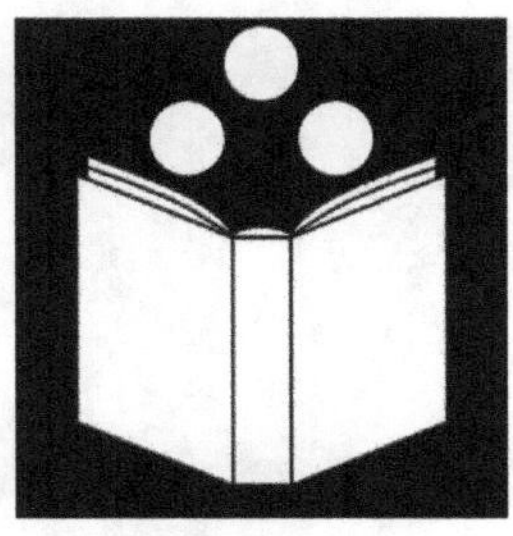

Origami per bambini
© 2017 Ciparum LLC
All rights reserved.
ISBN:1-63589-513-8
ISBN:978-1-63589-513-1

www.youngscholar.co

Origami para ninos

Sommario

Orso

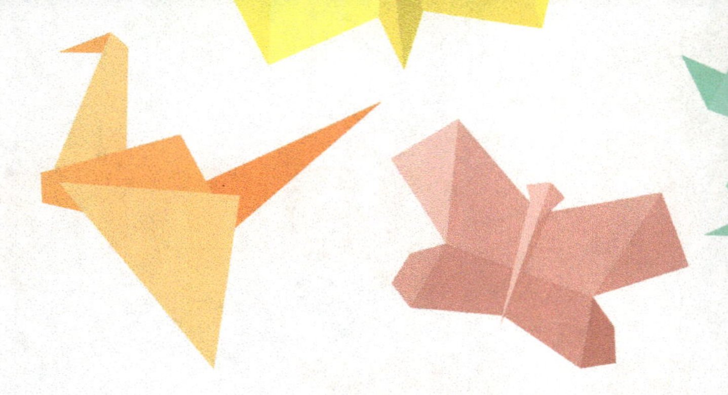

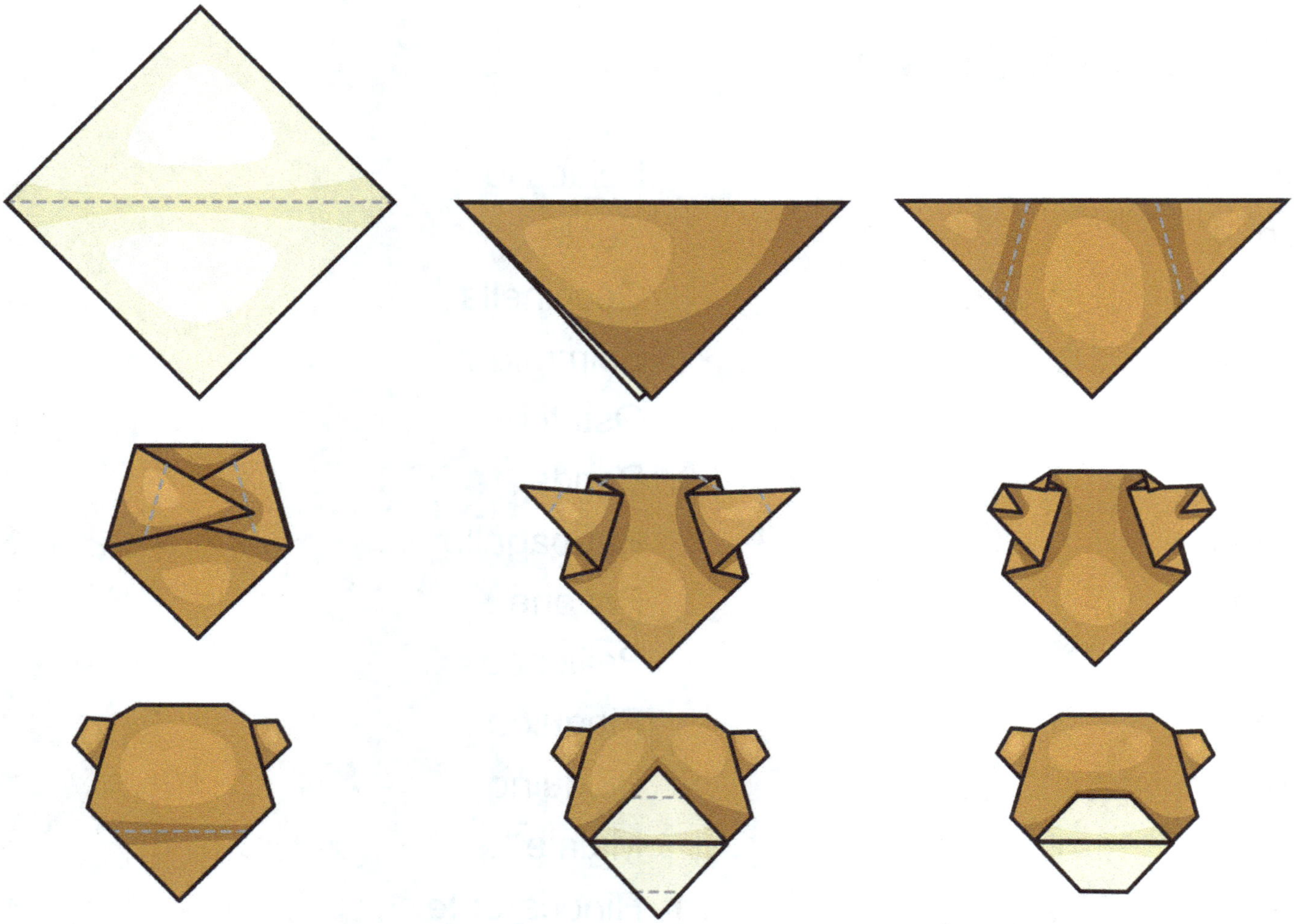

Bear

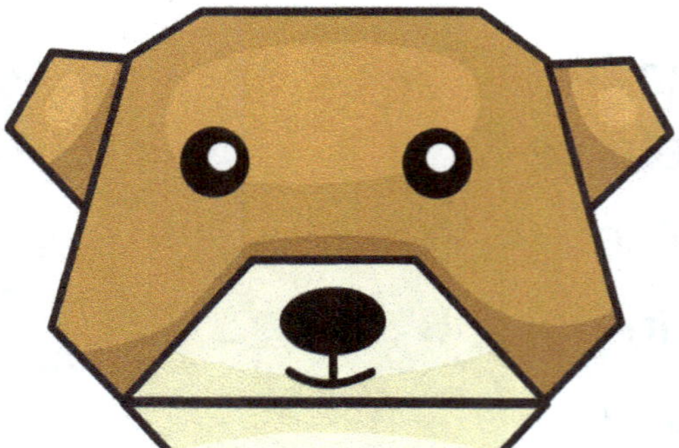

Ape

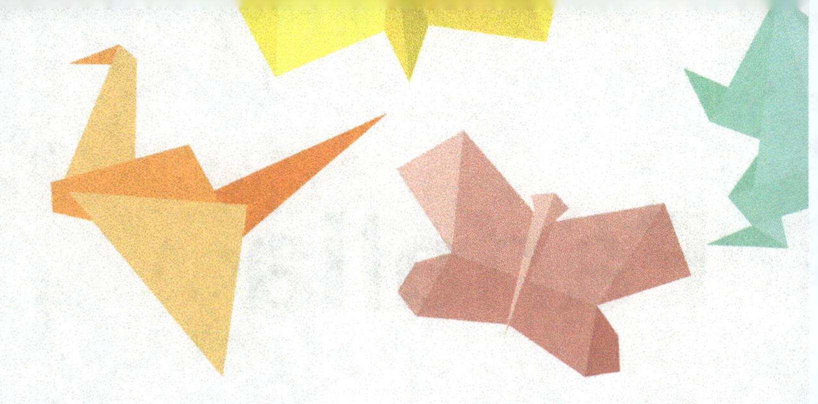

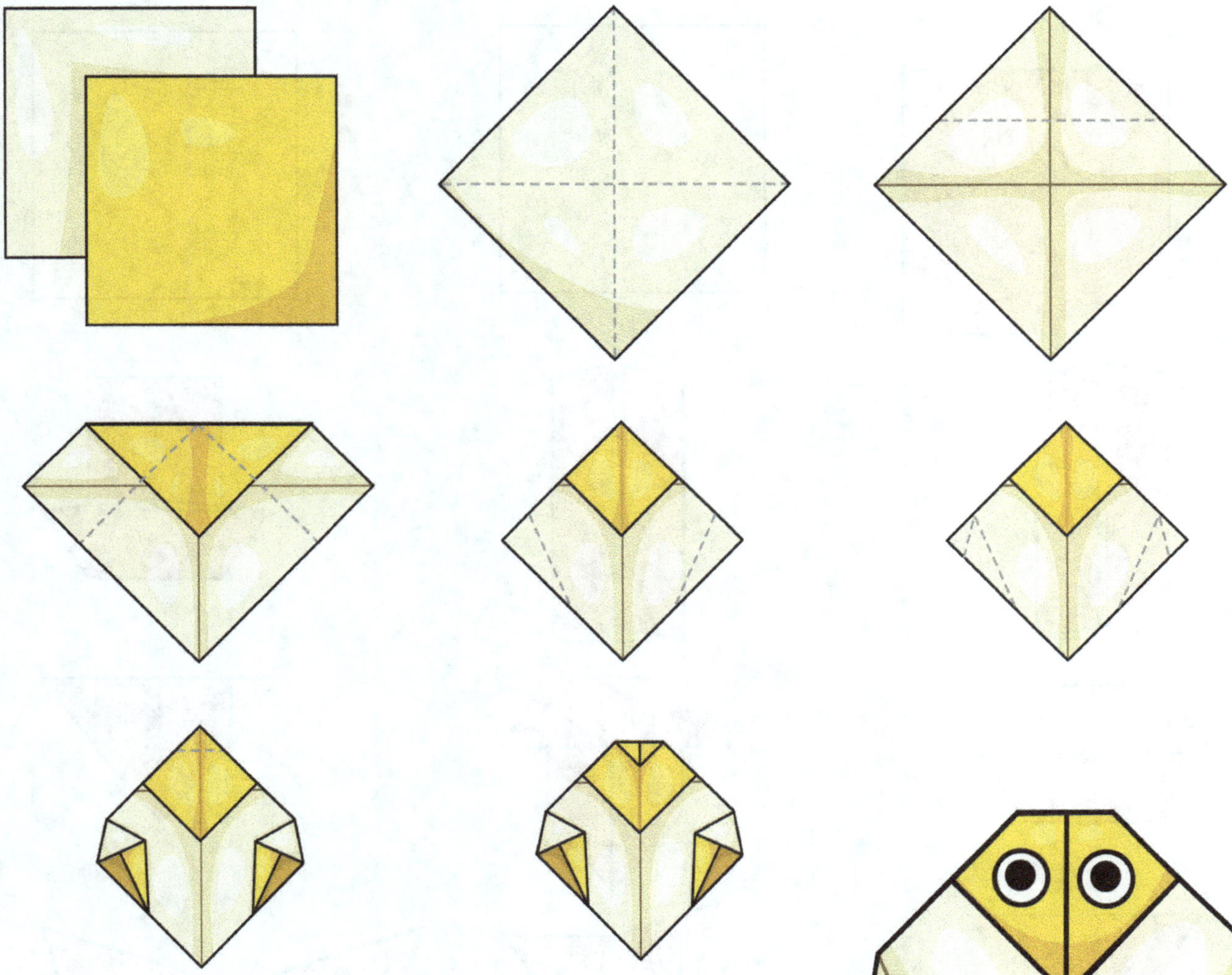

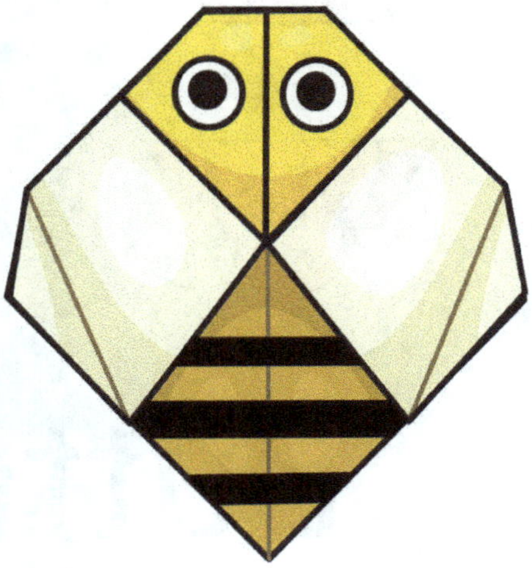

Bee

Farfalla

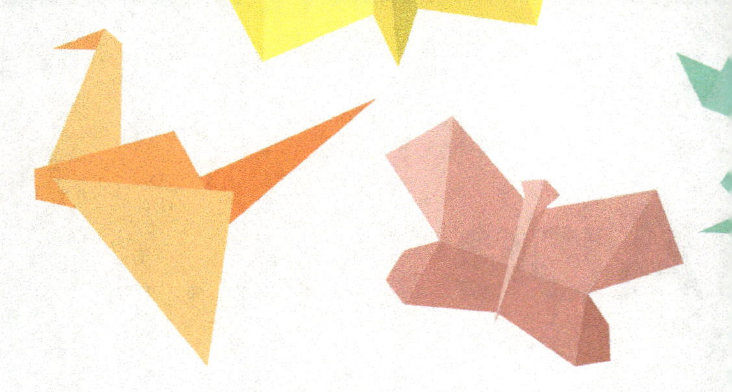

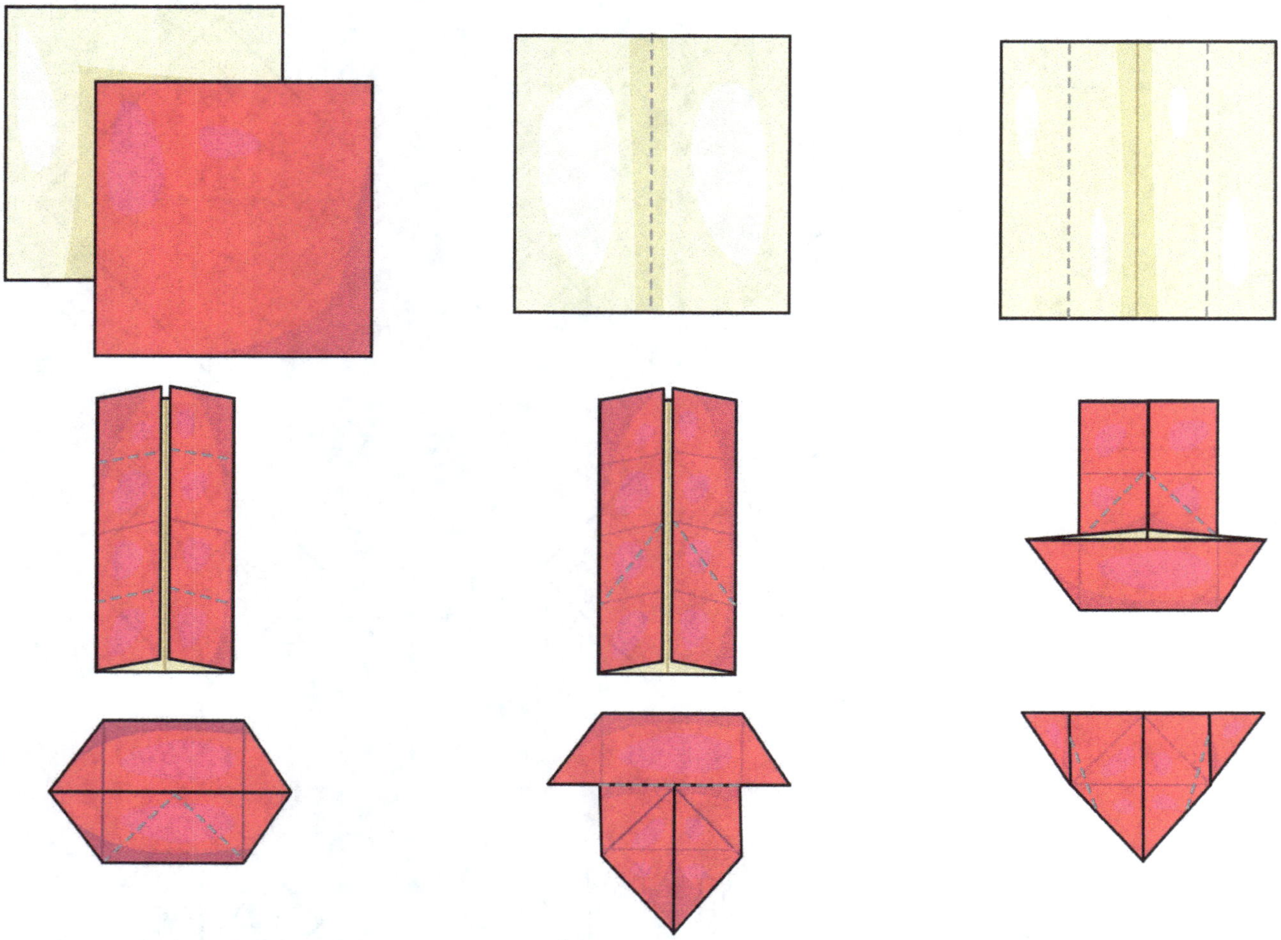

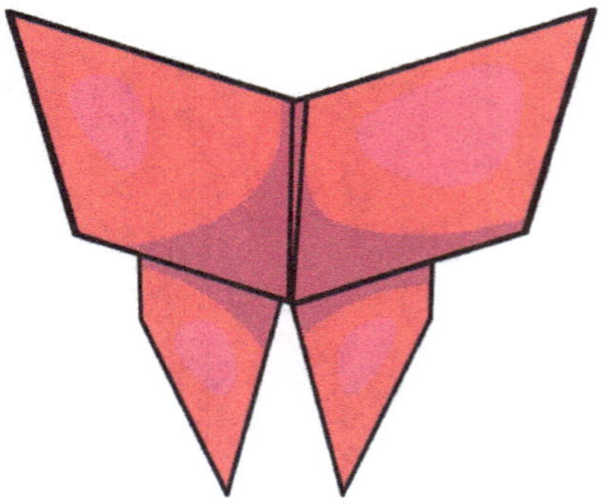

Butterfly

Gatto

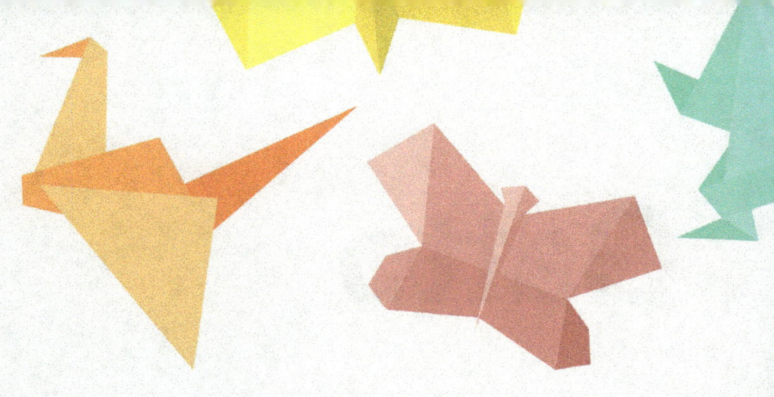

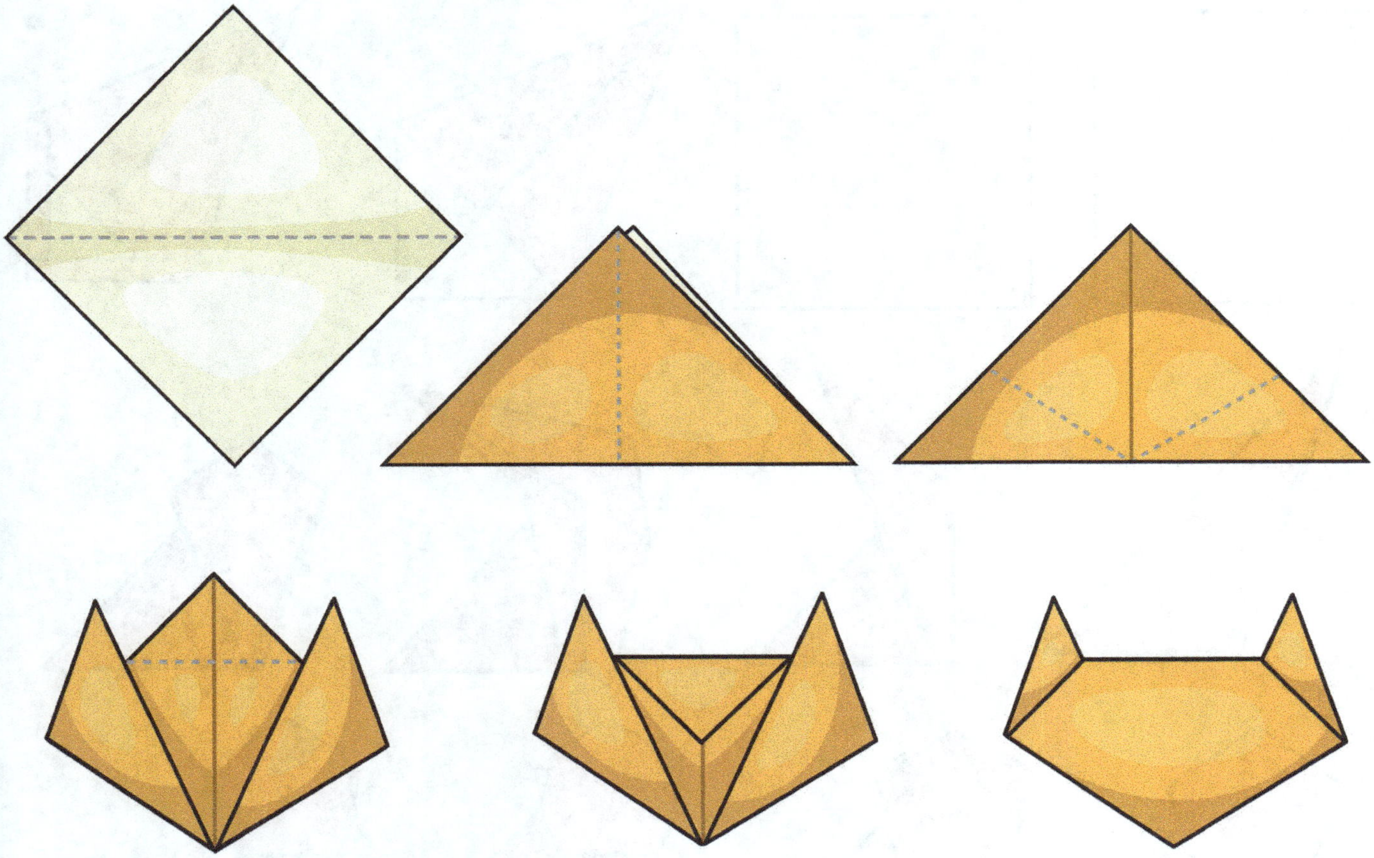

Cat

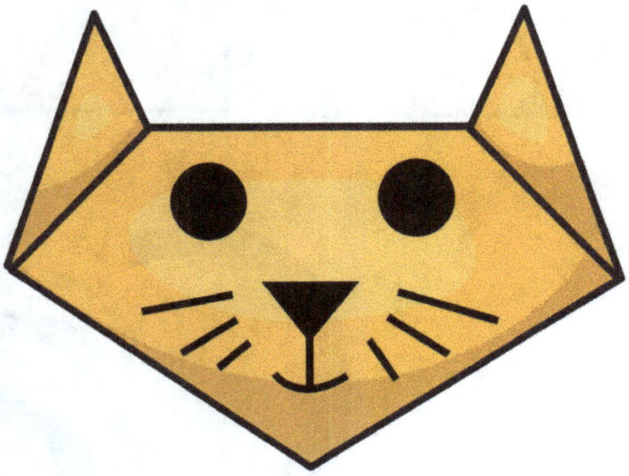

Gatto

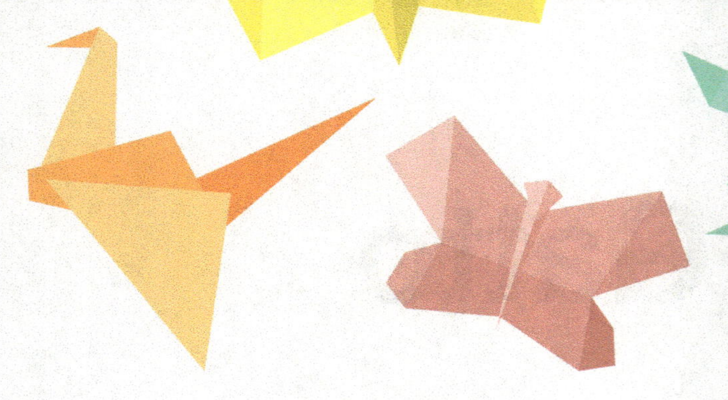

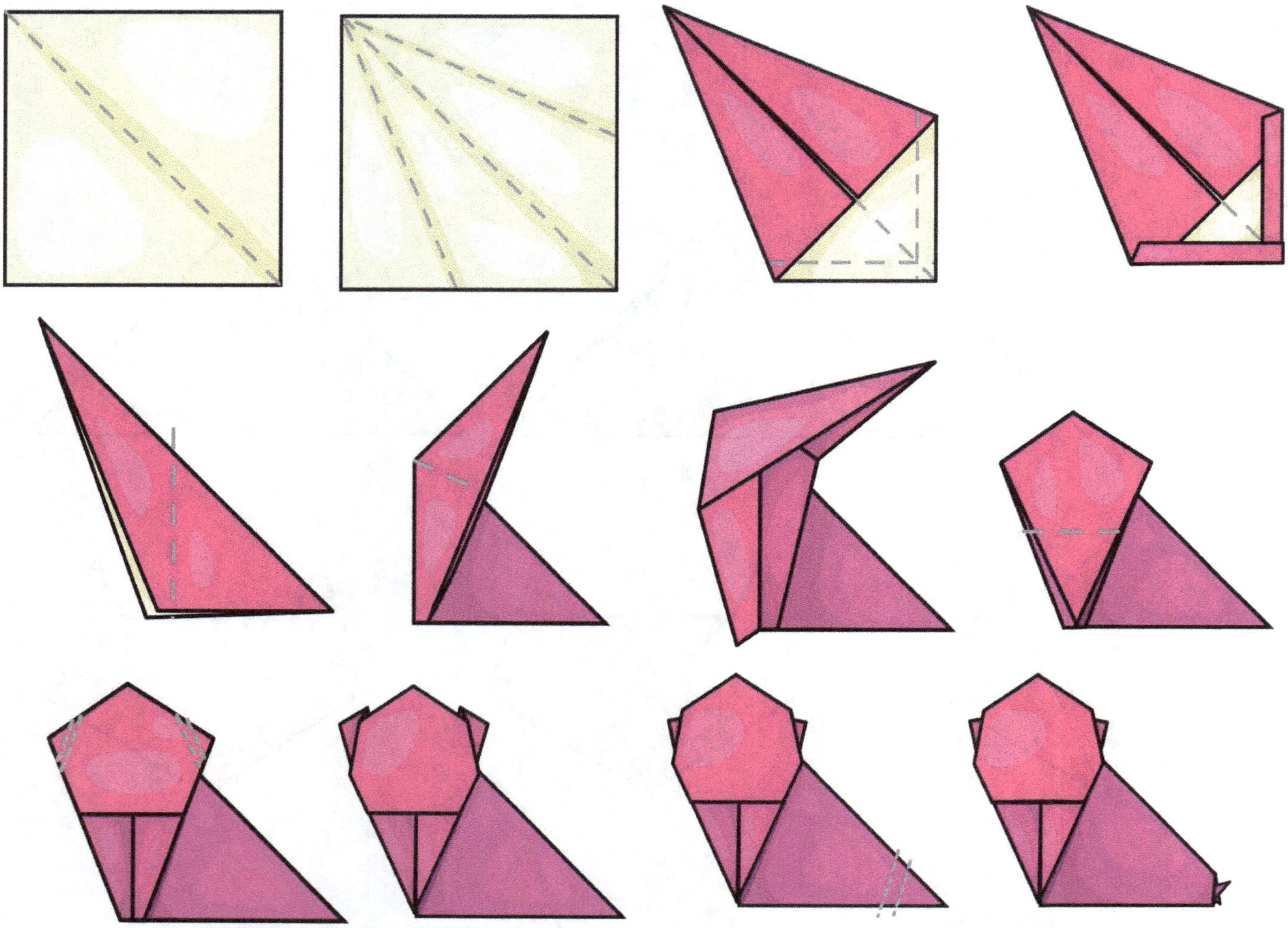

Cat

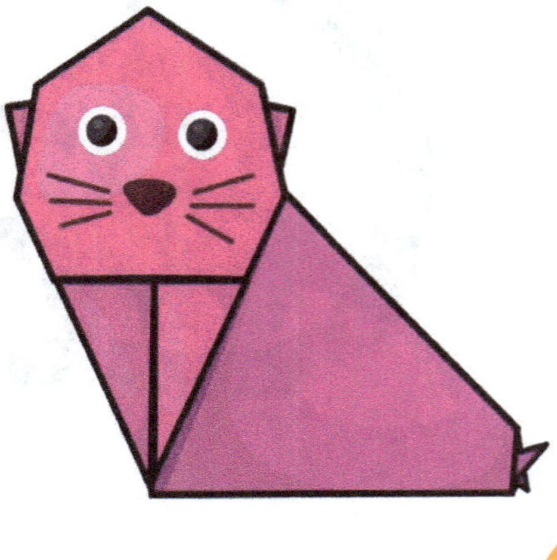

Pulcino

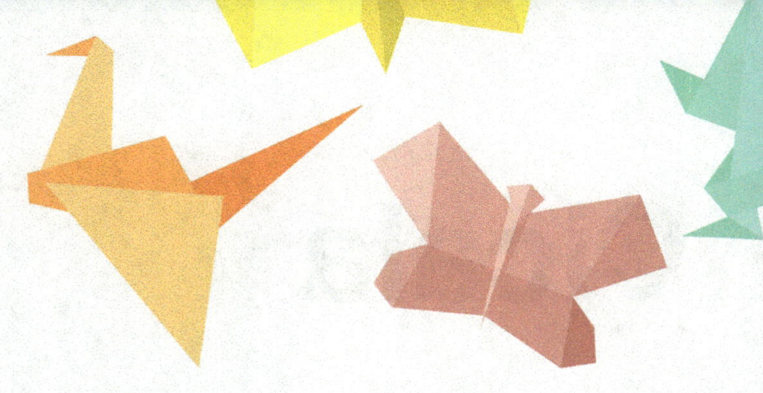

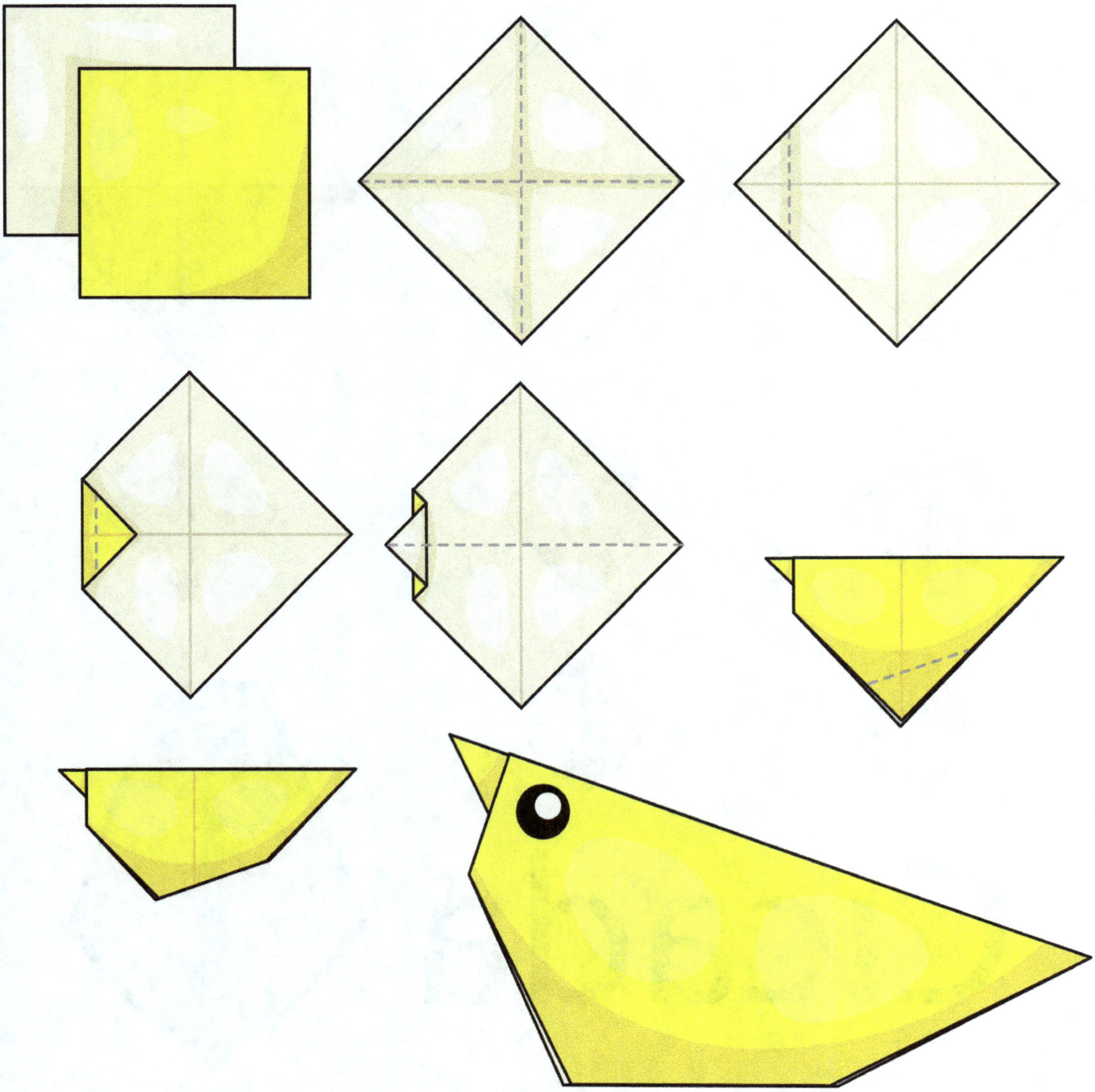

Cicala

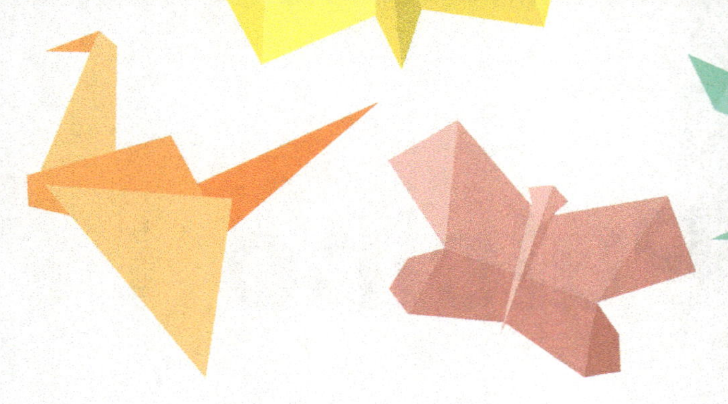

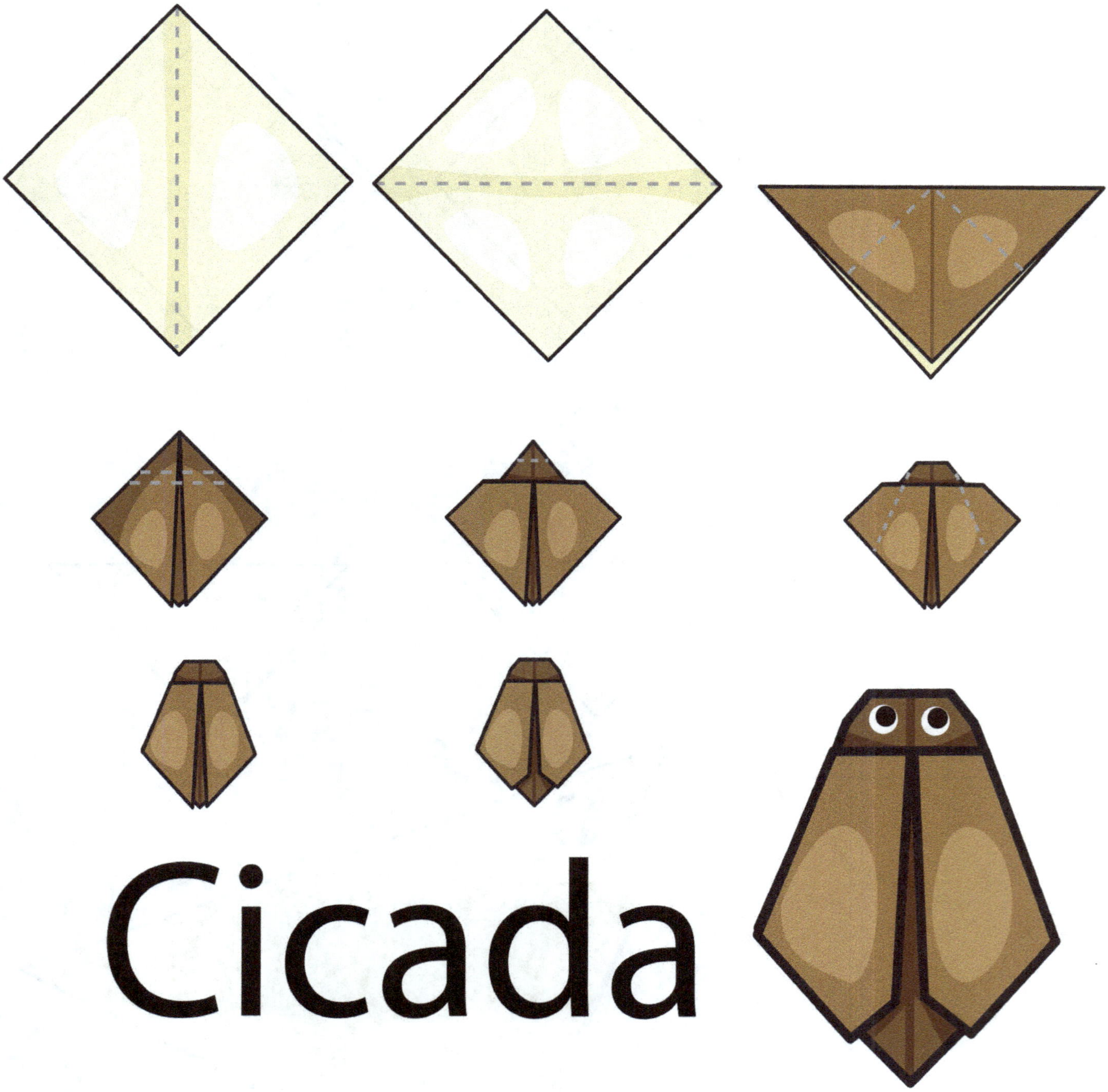

Cicada

Mucca

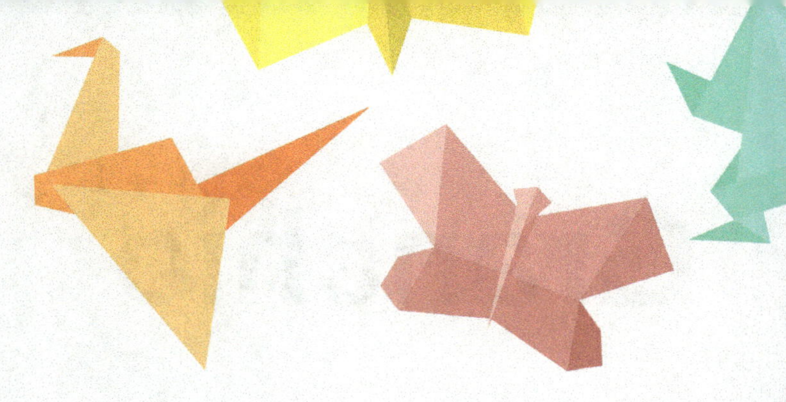

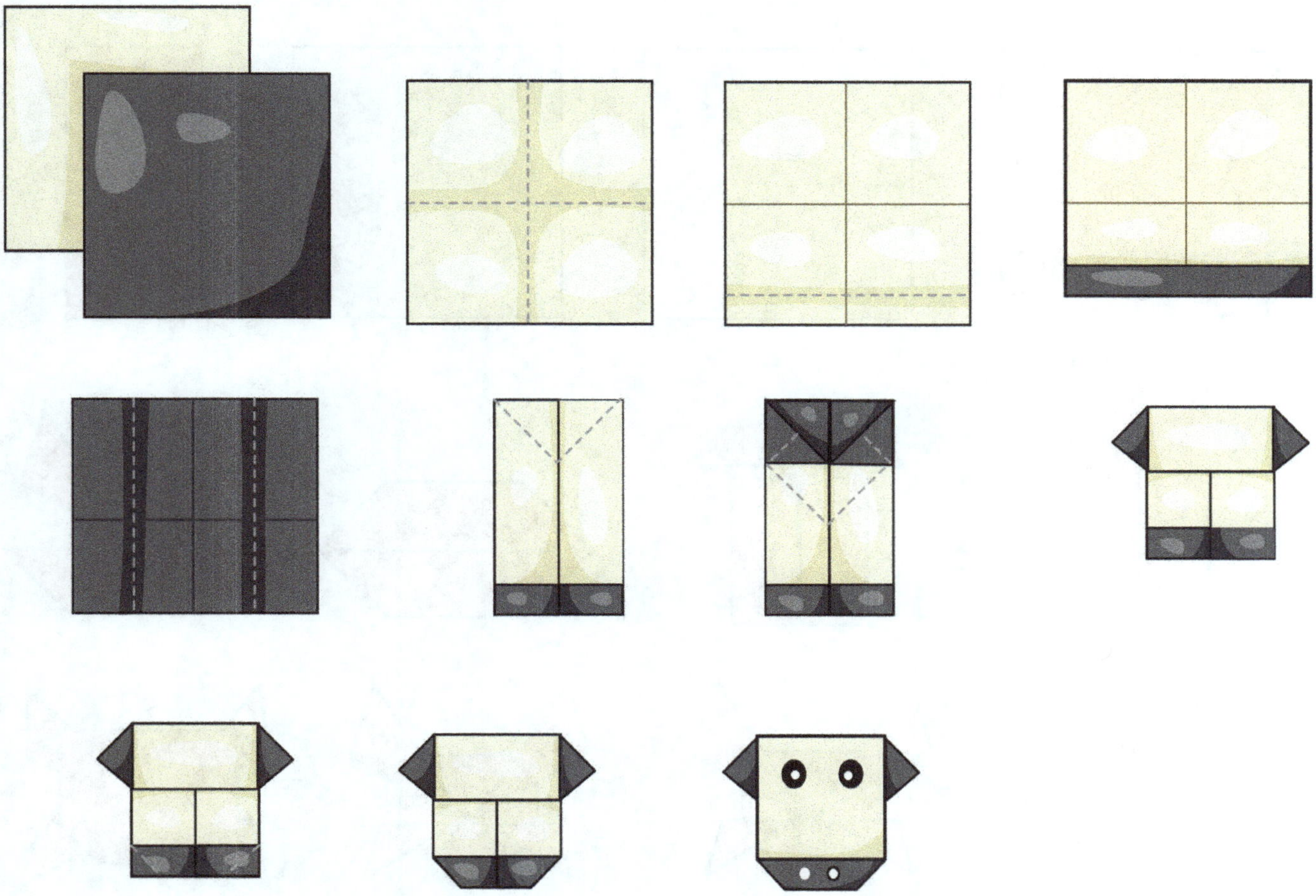

Cow

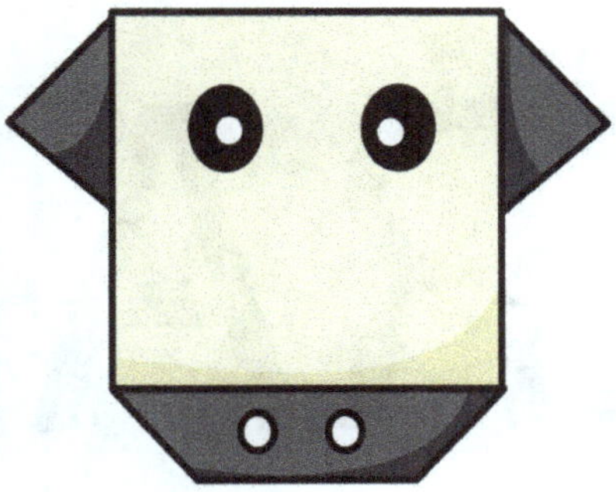

Granchio

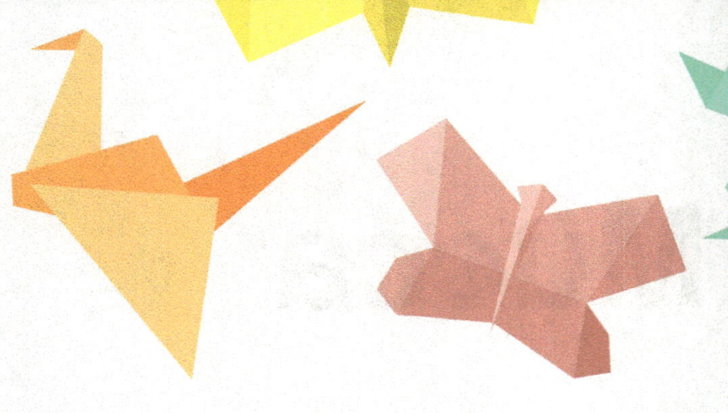

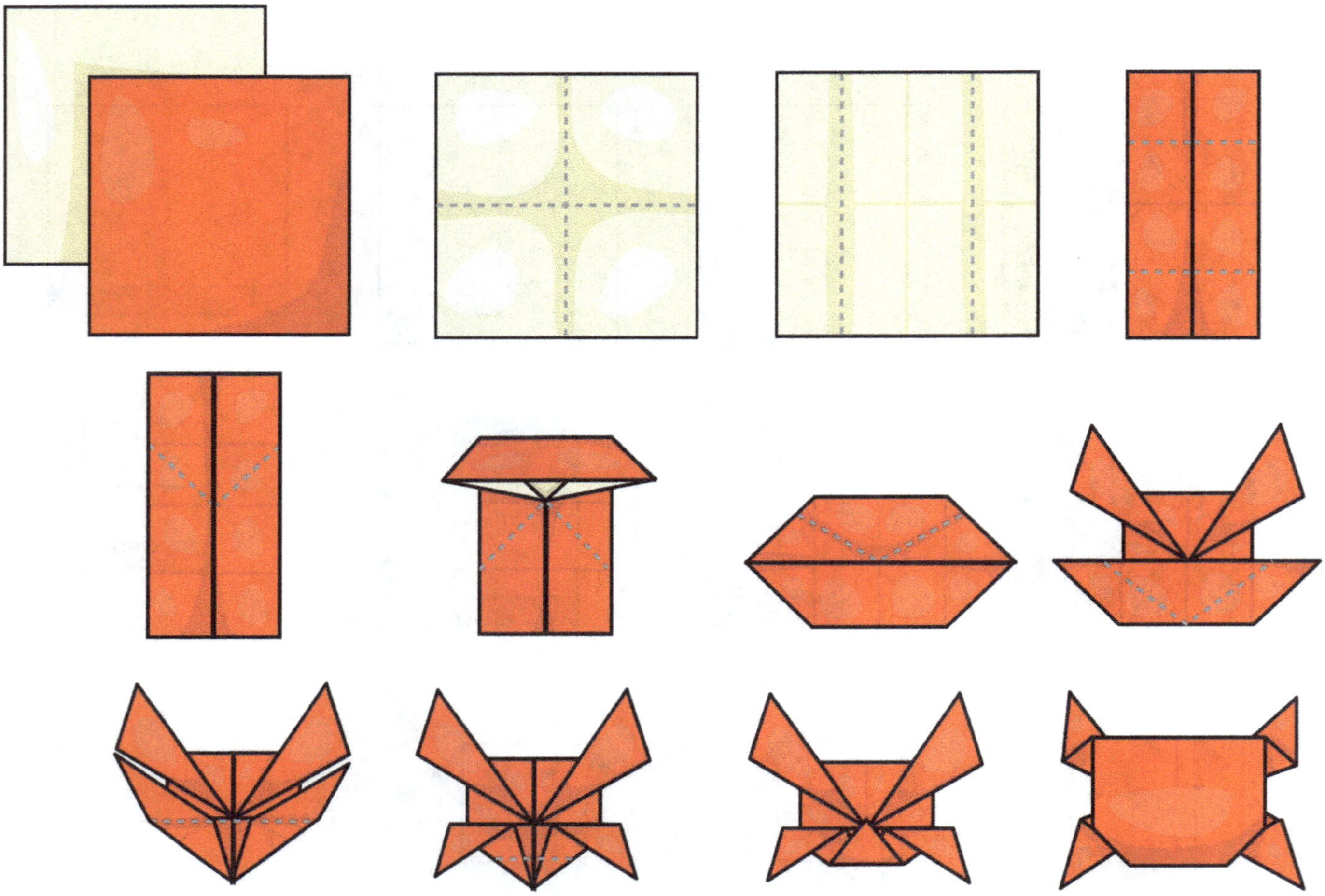

CRAB

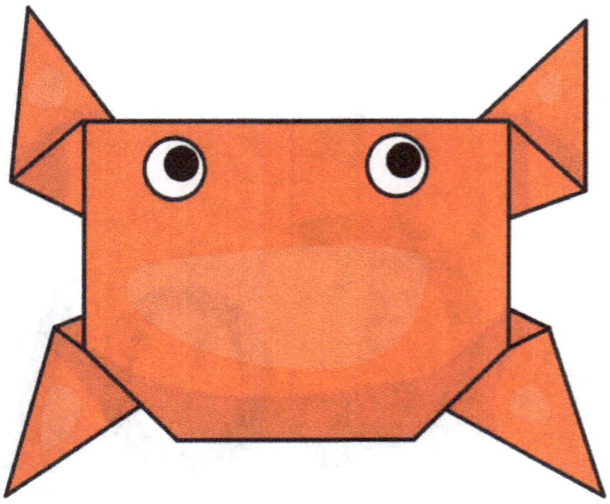

Corvo

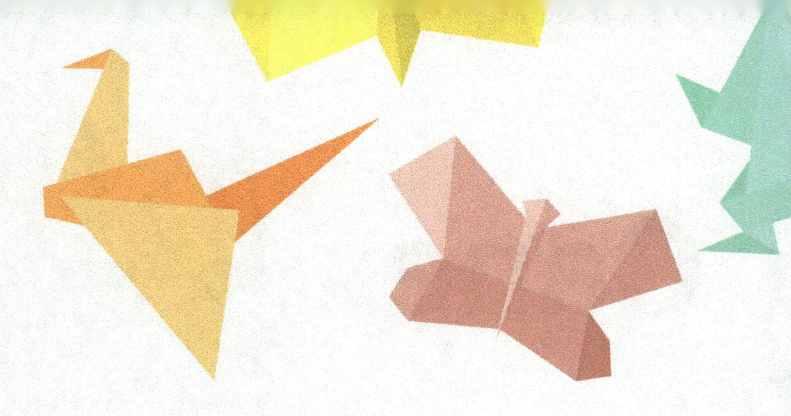

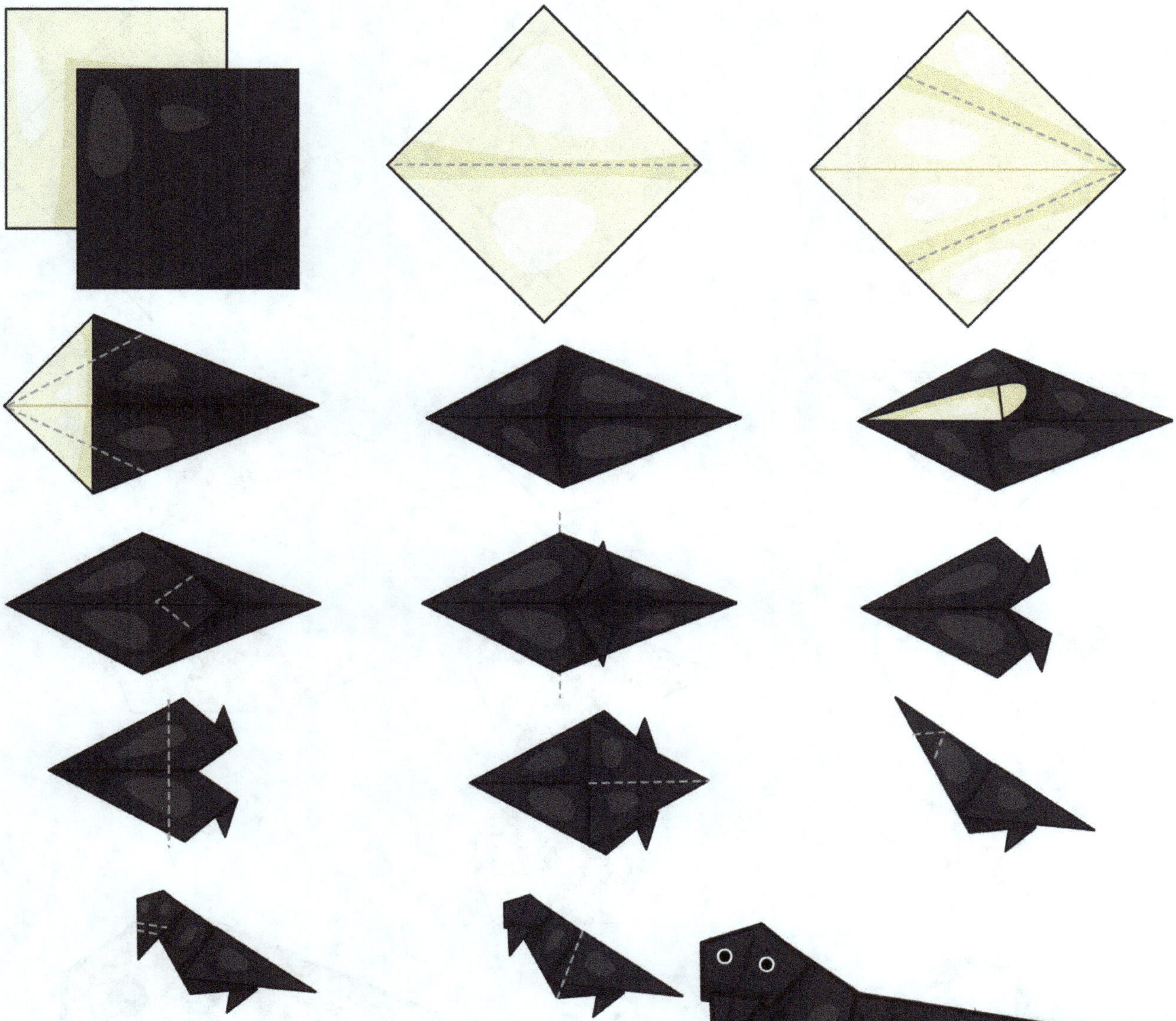

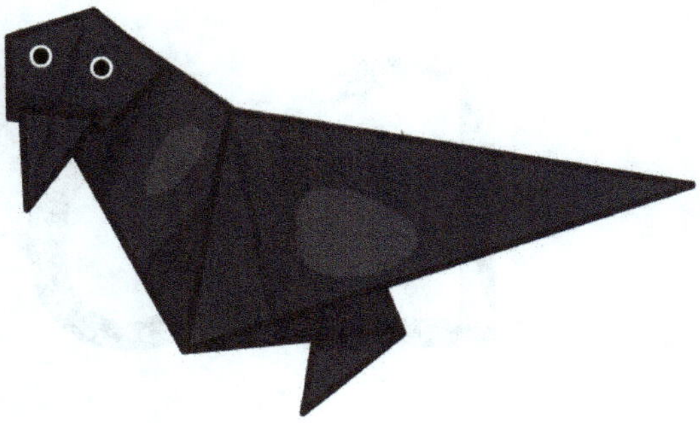

Crow

Cane

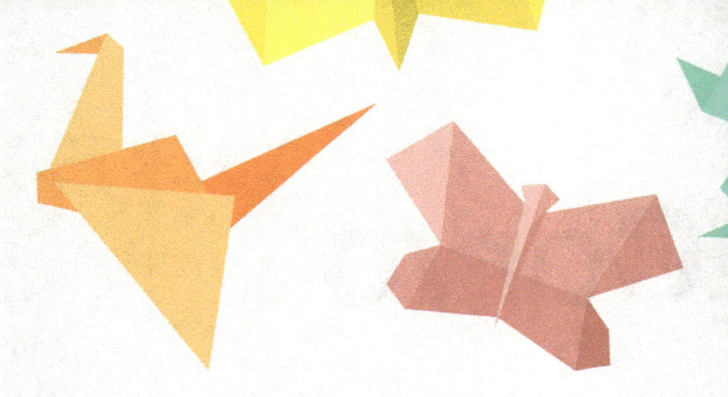

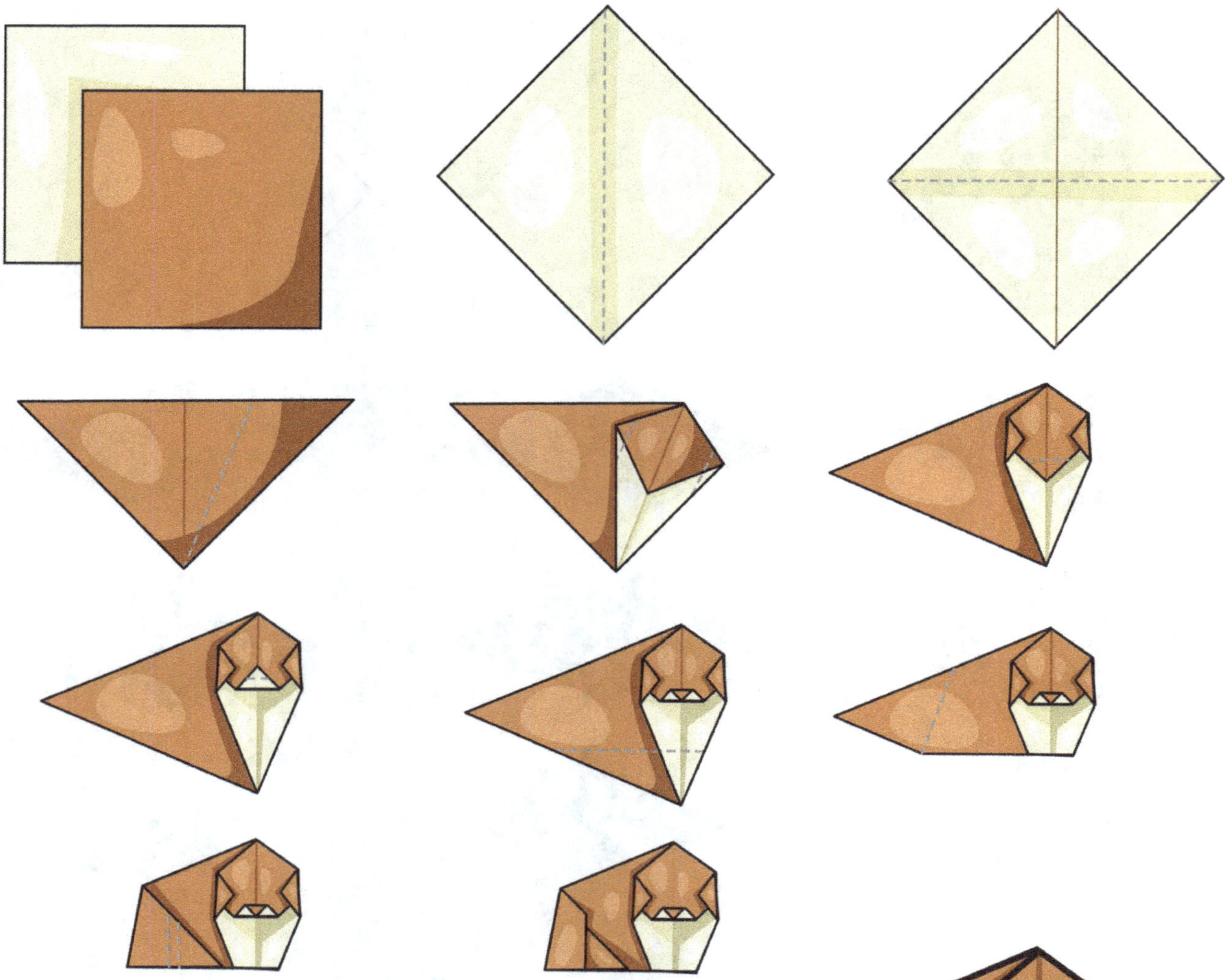

Dog

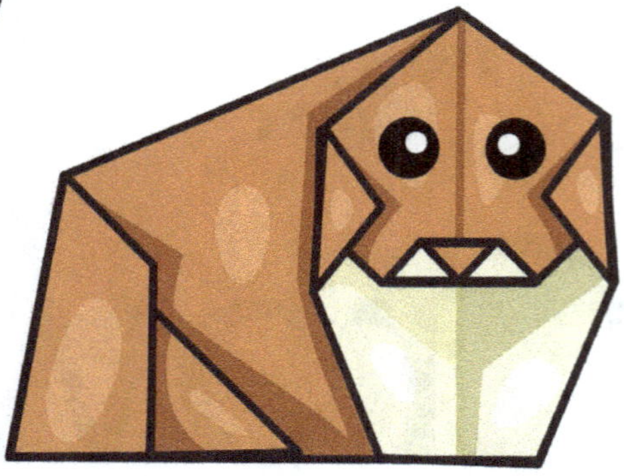

Anatra

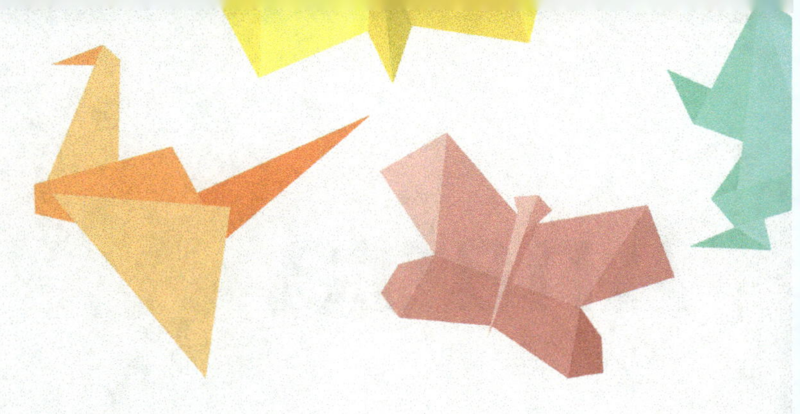

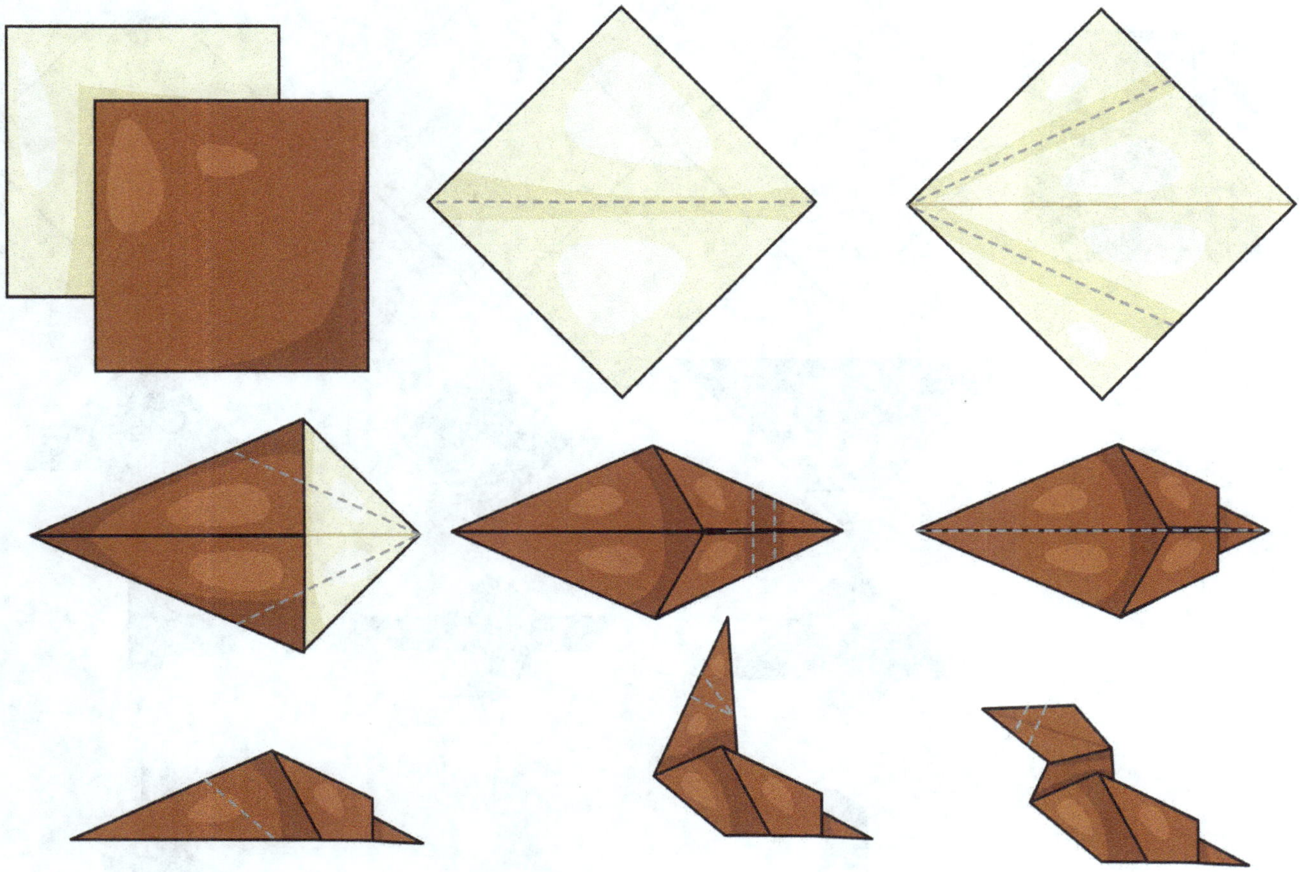

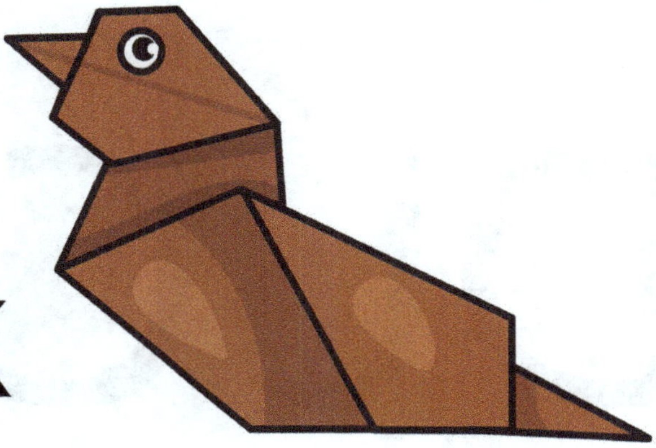

Wild Duck

Anatra

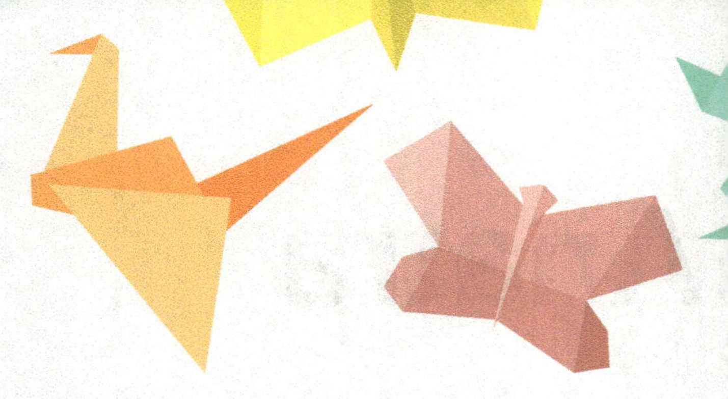

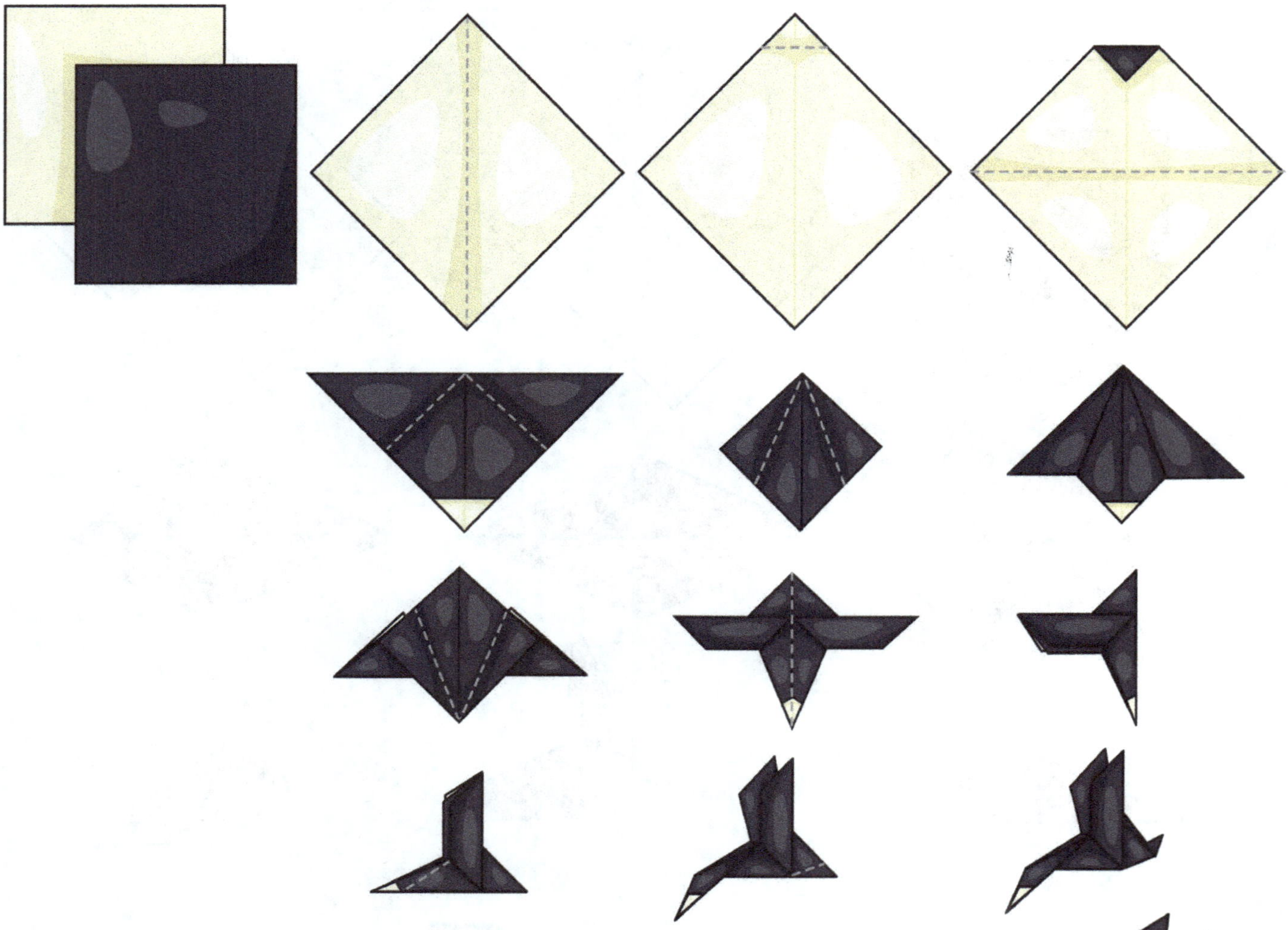

DUCK

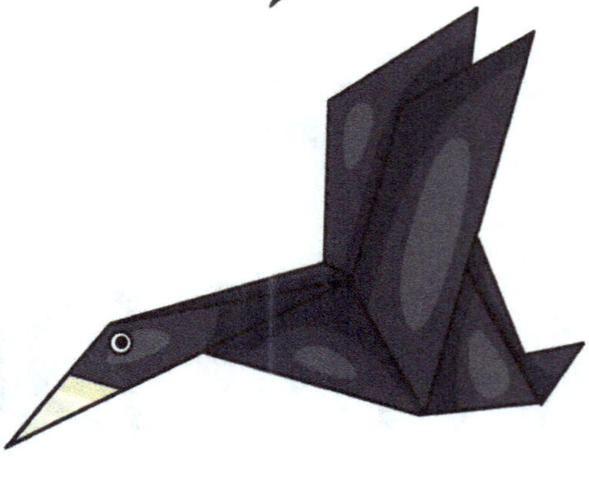

Elefante

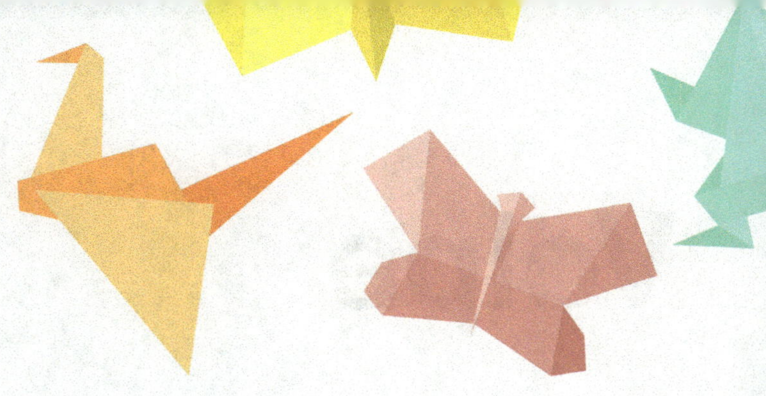

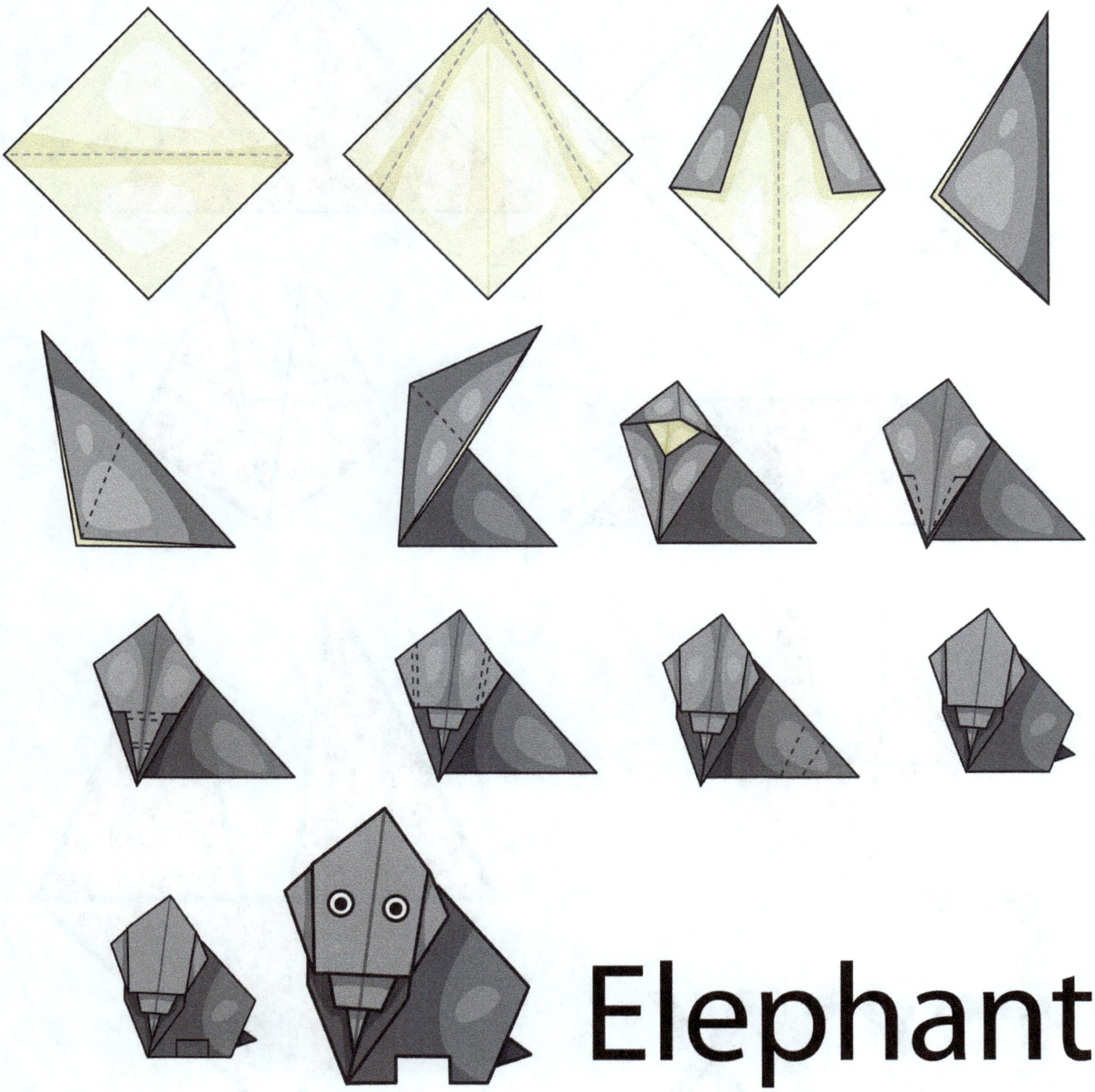

Elephant

Volpe

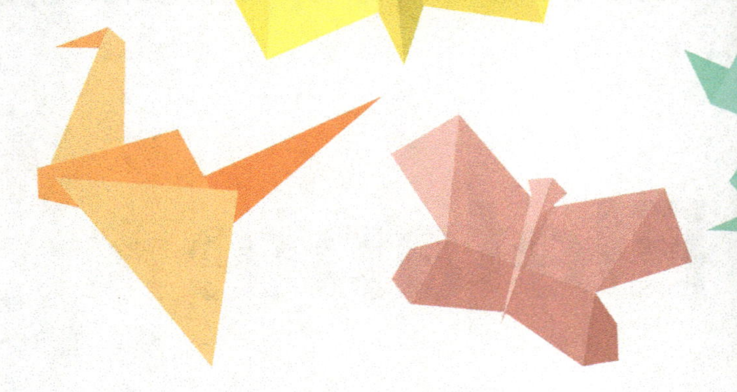

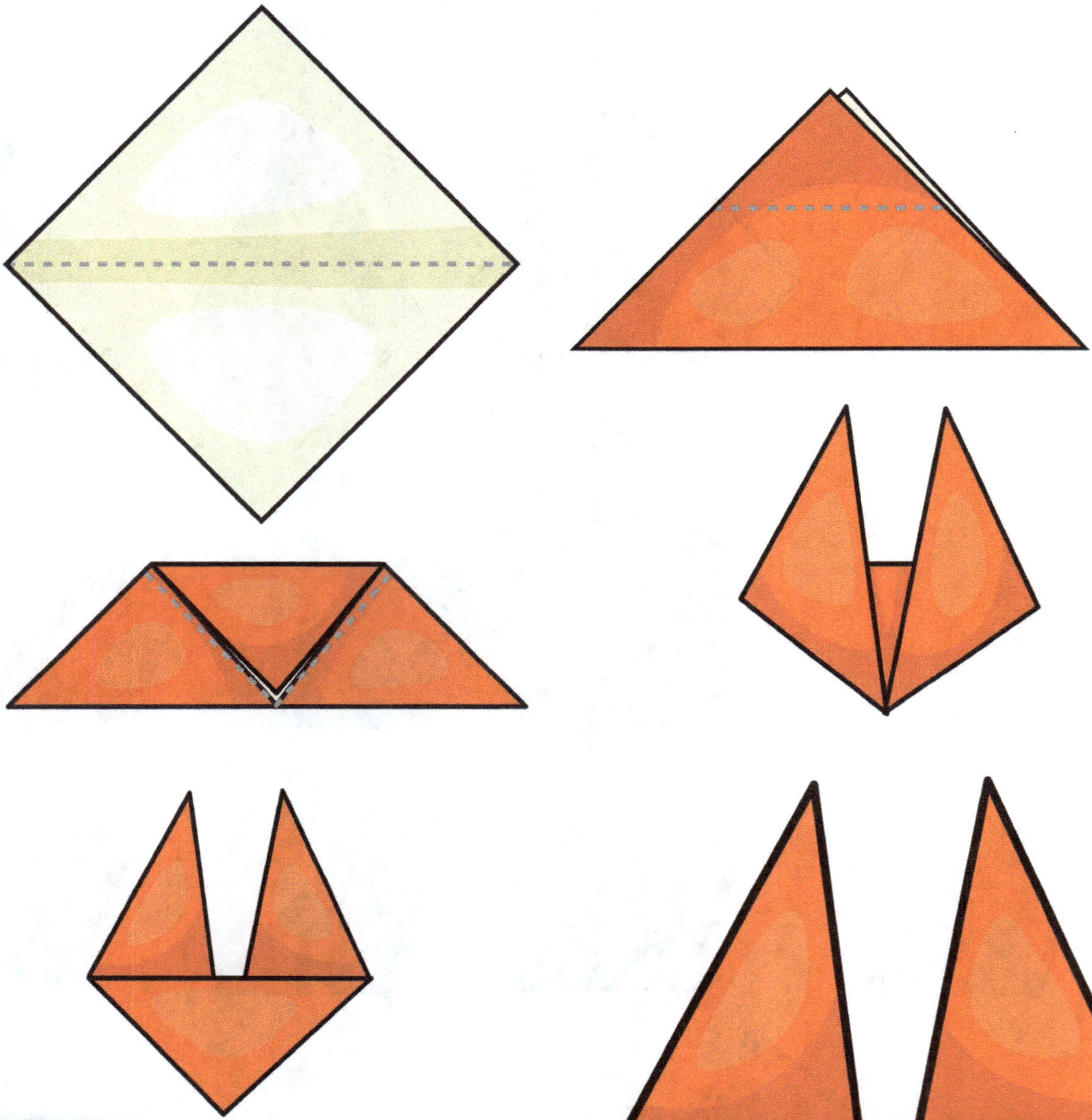

Fox

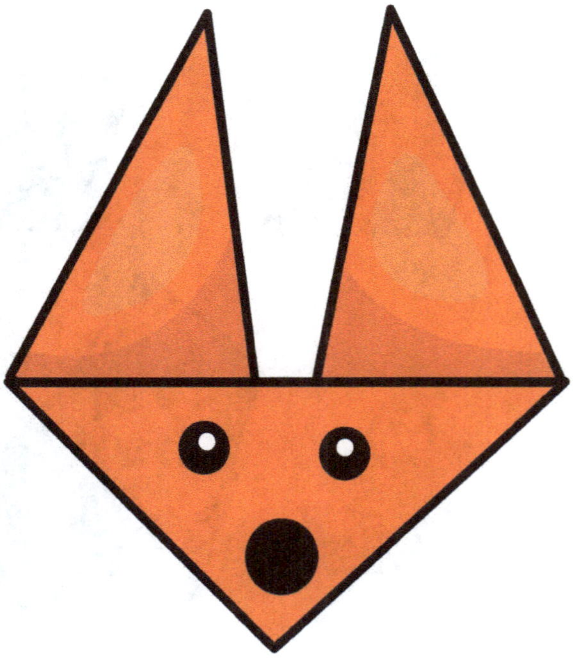

Volpe

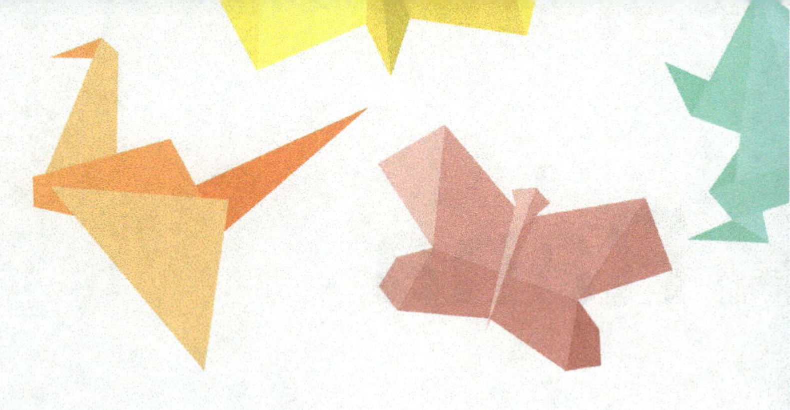

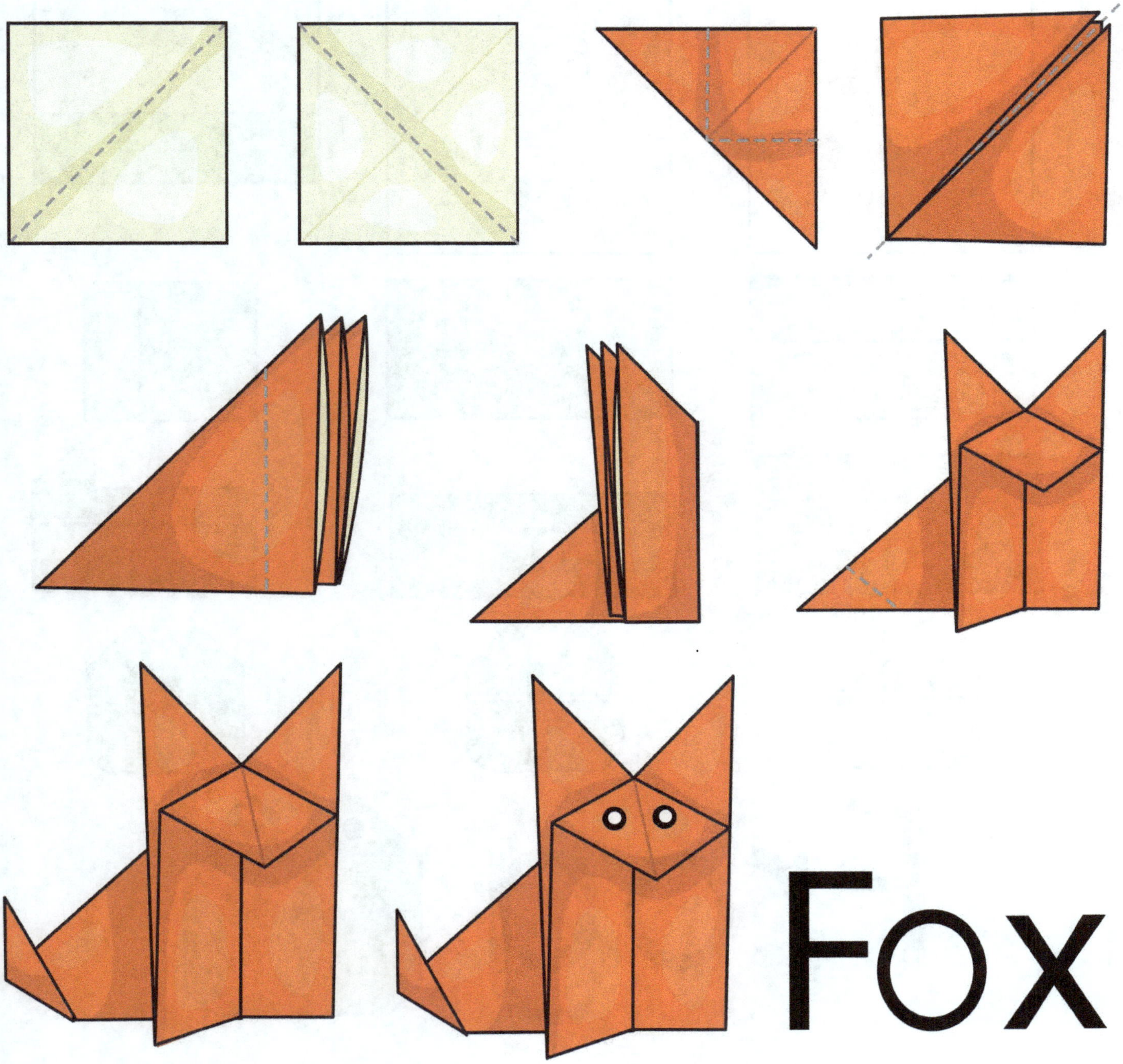

Fox

Rana

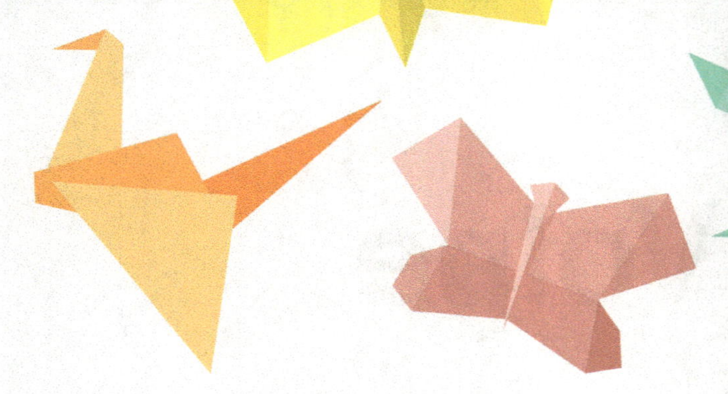

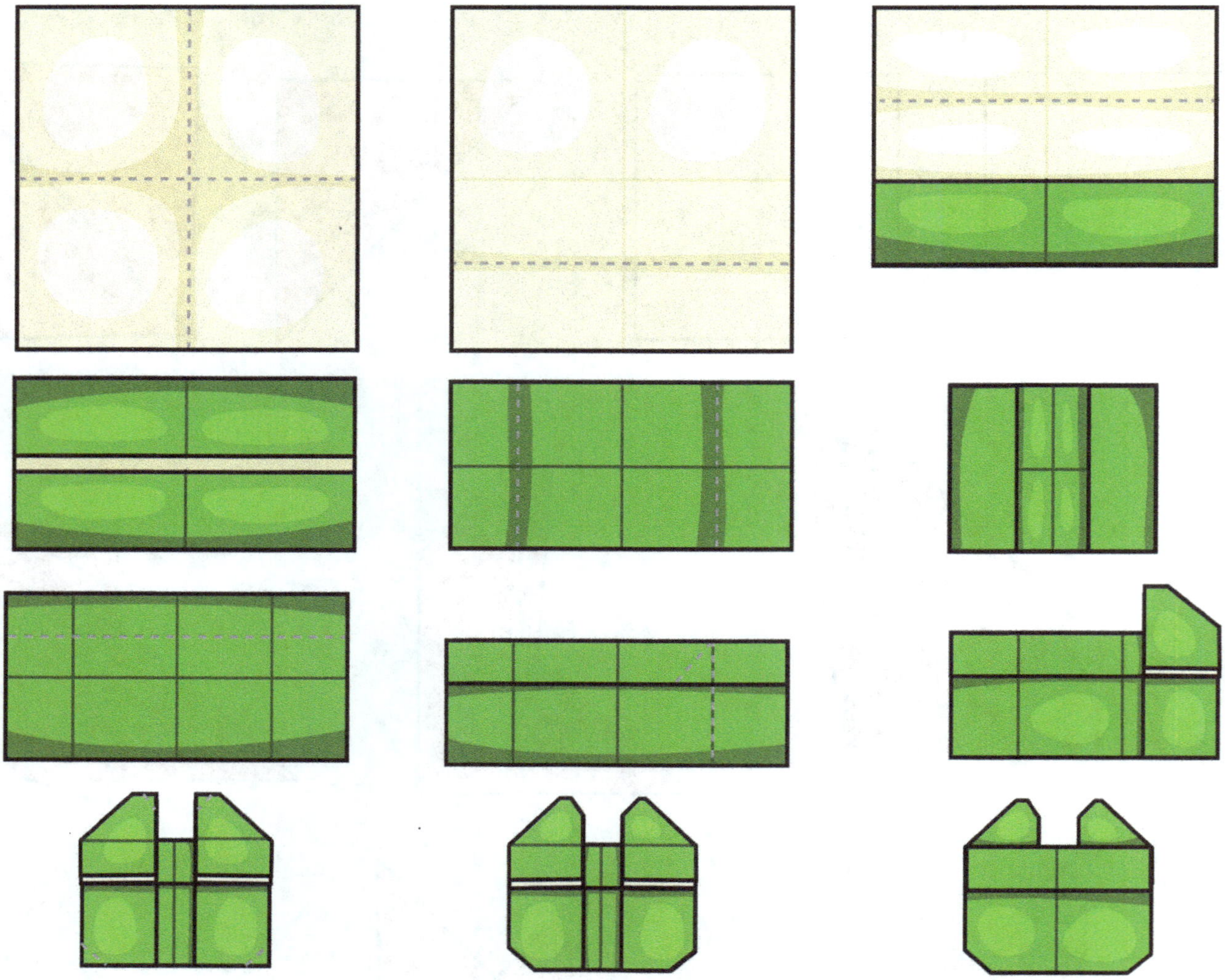

Frog

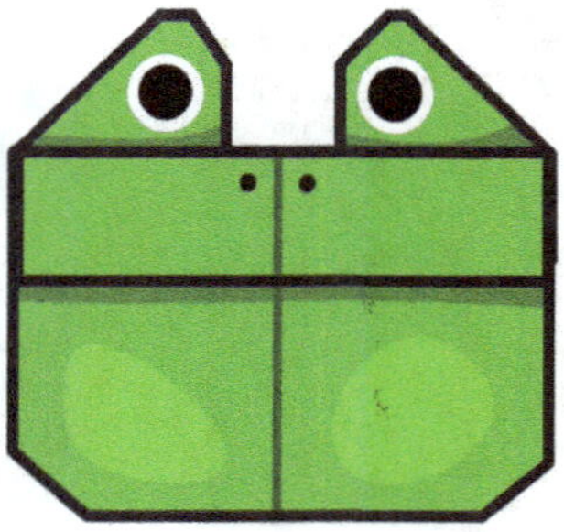

Giraffa

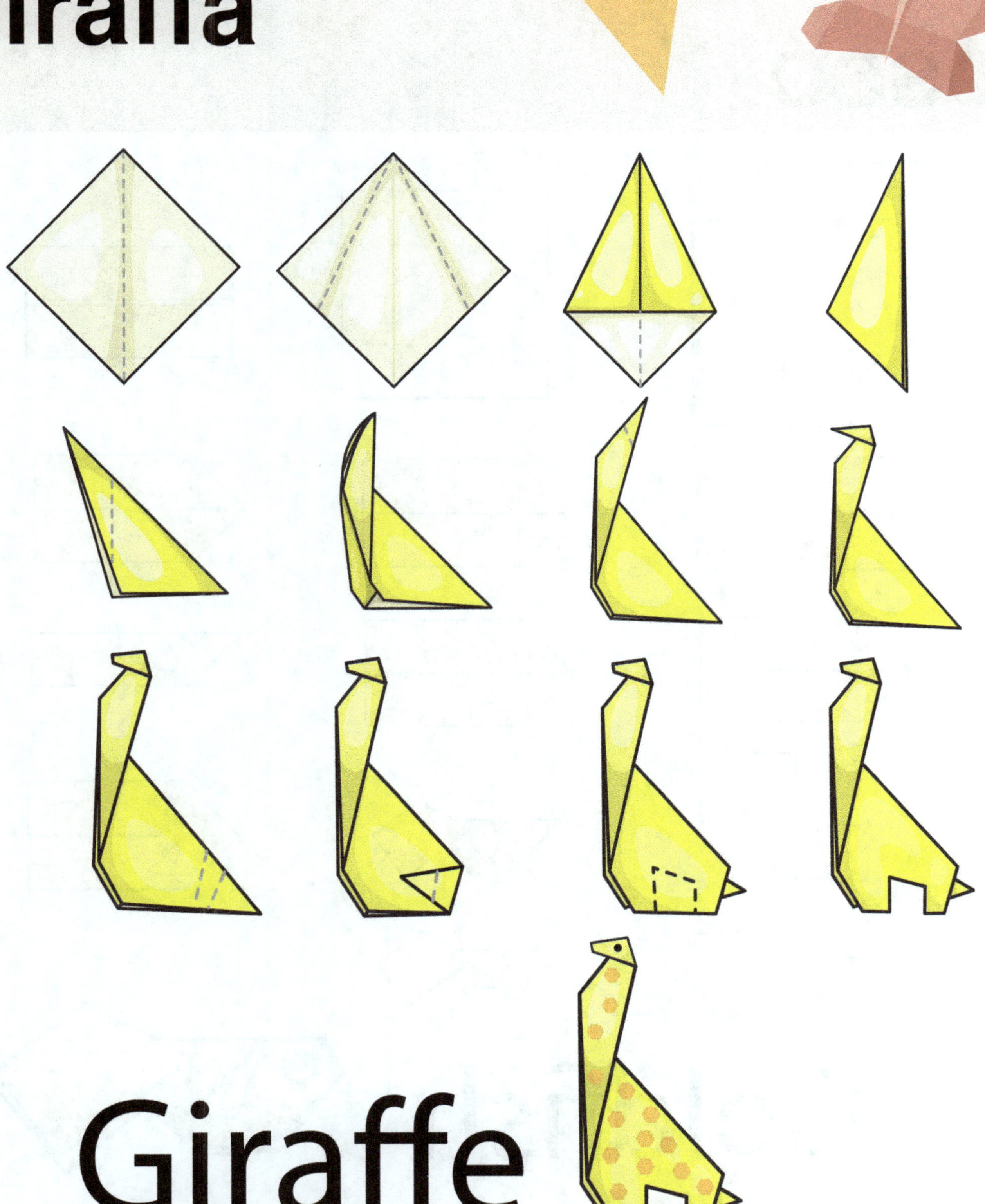

Giraffe

pesce rosso

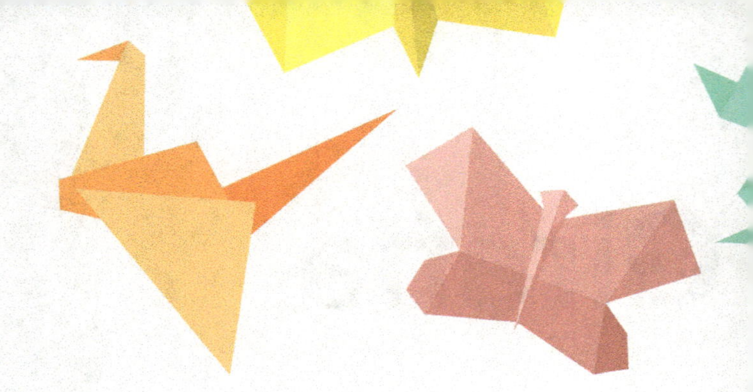

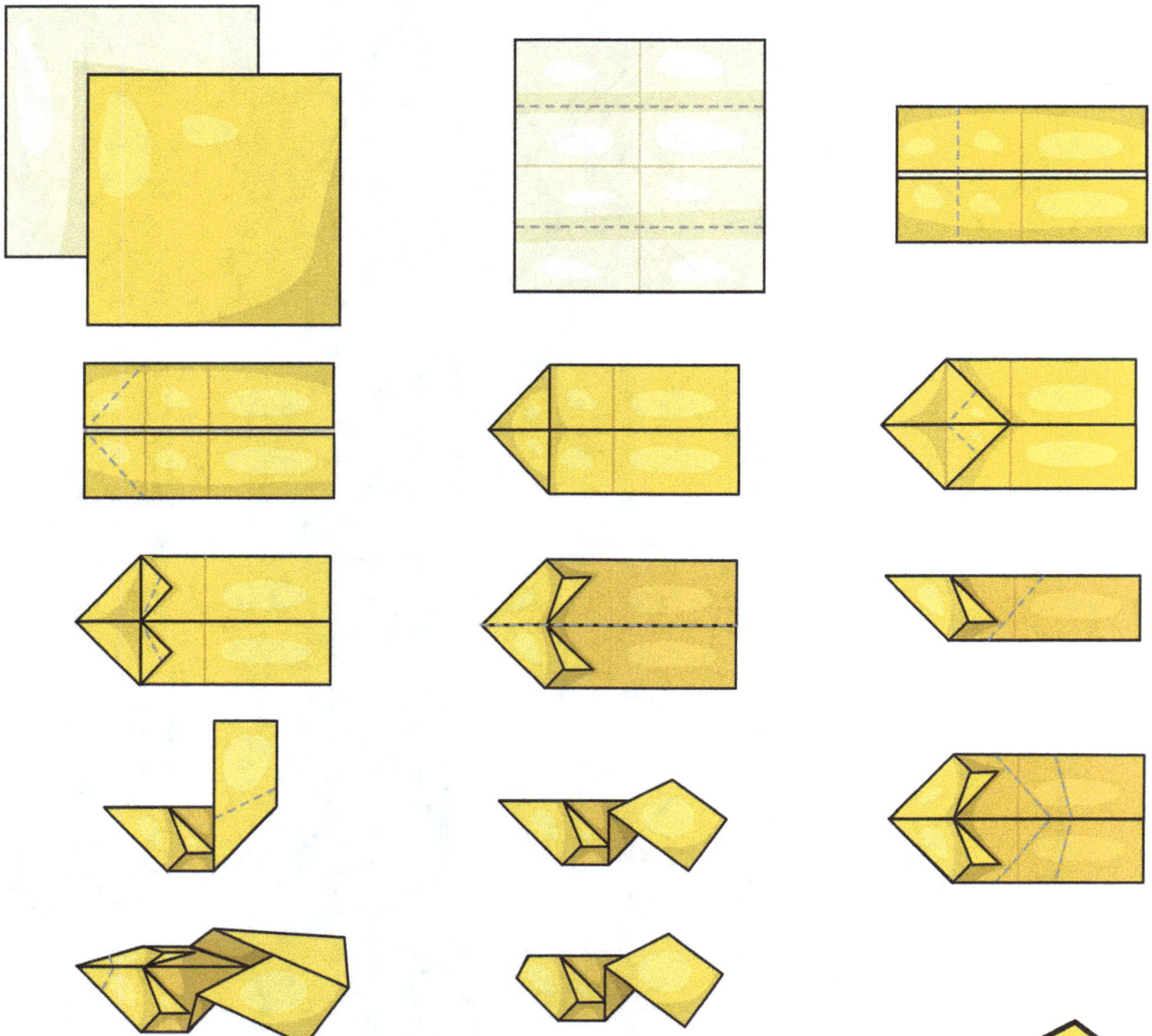

Goldfish

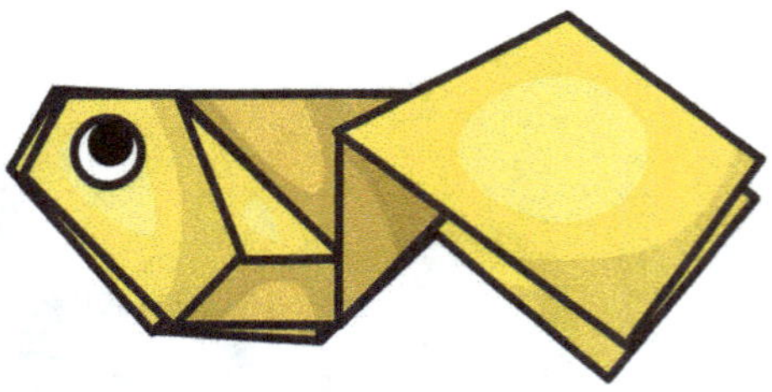

Criceto

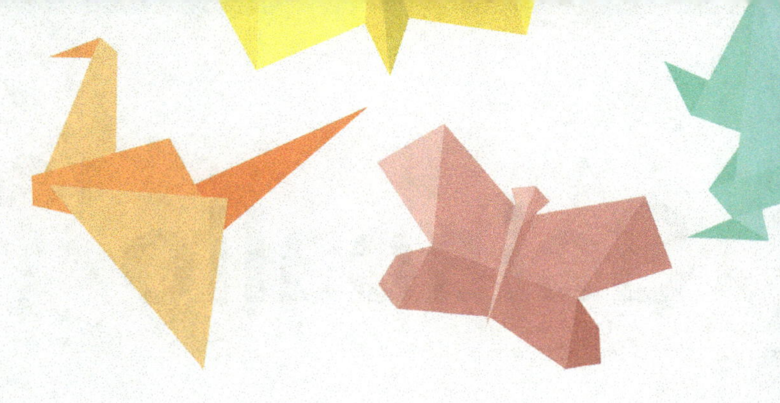

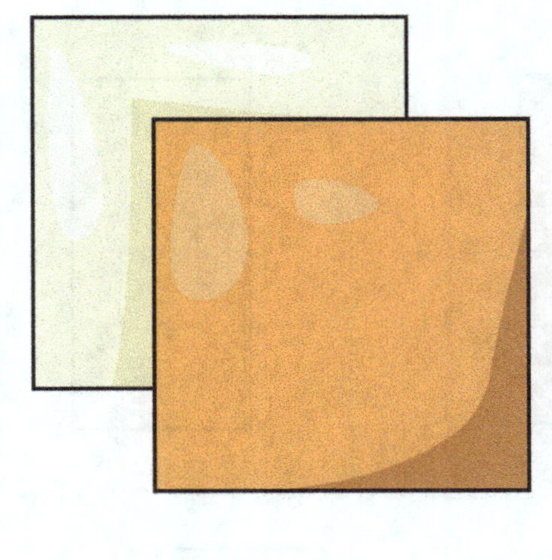

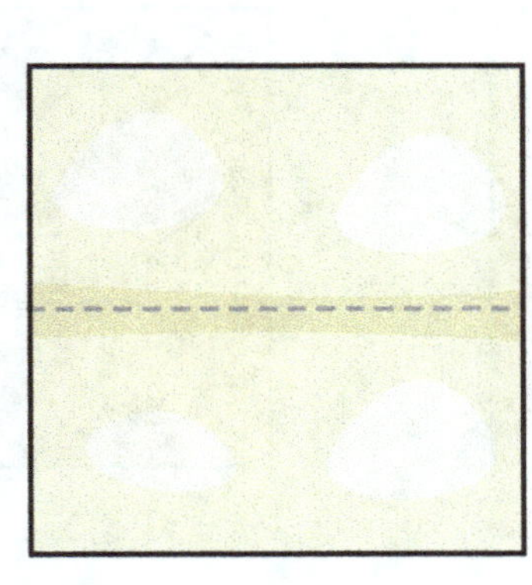

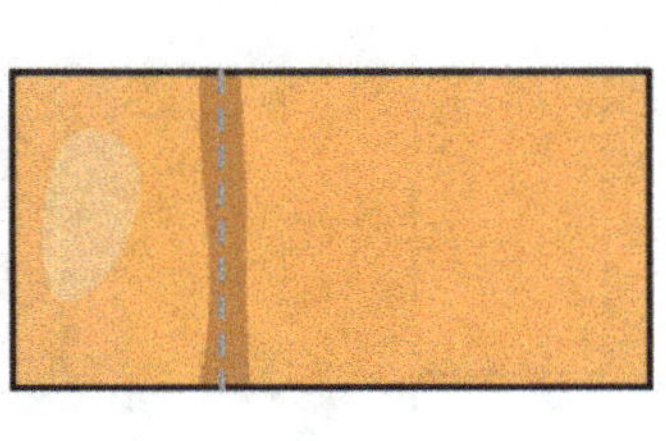

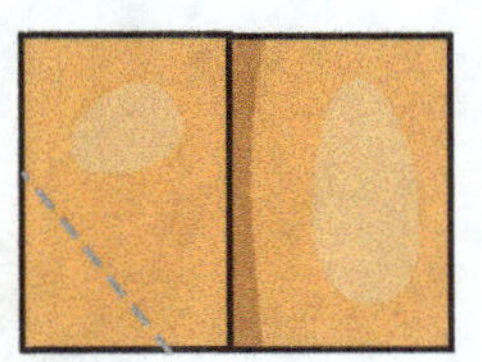

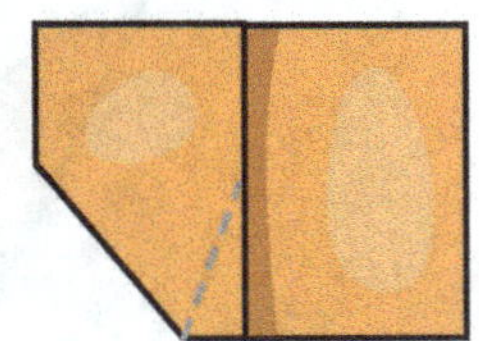

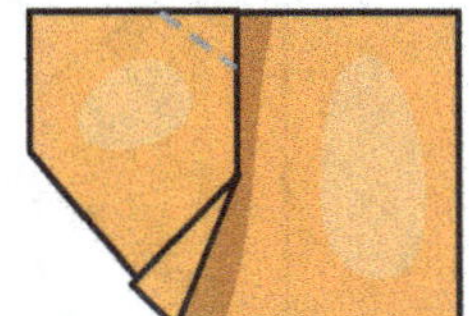

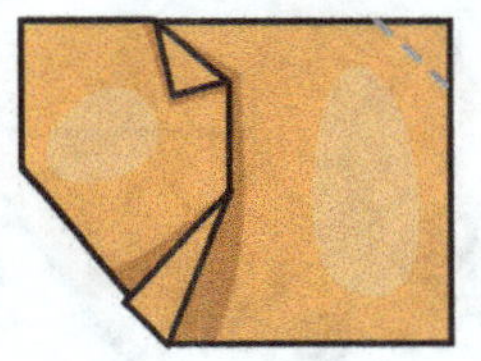

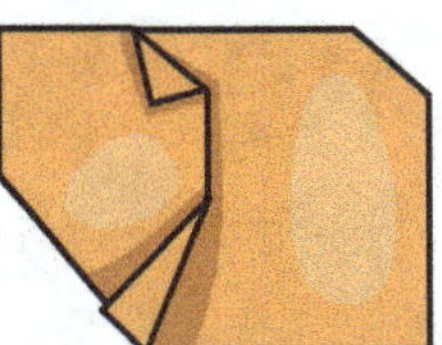

Hamster 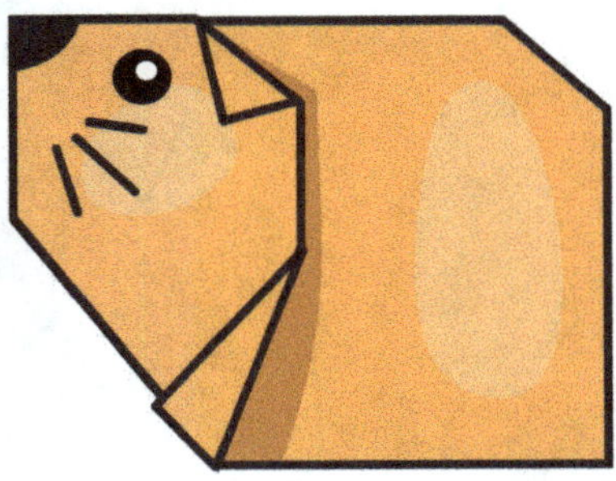

Sciacallo

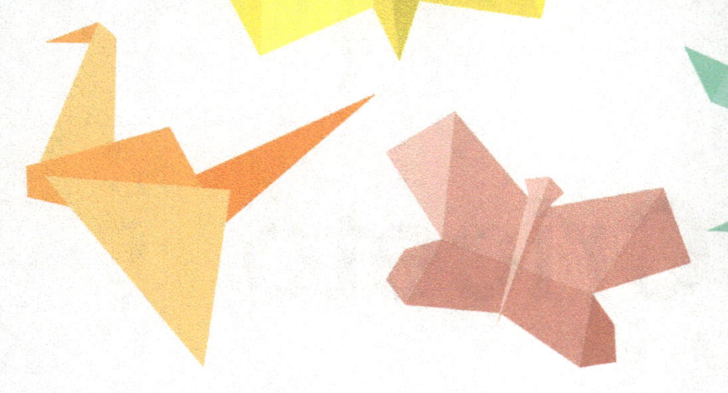

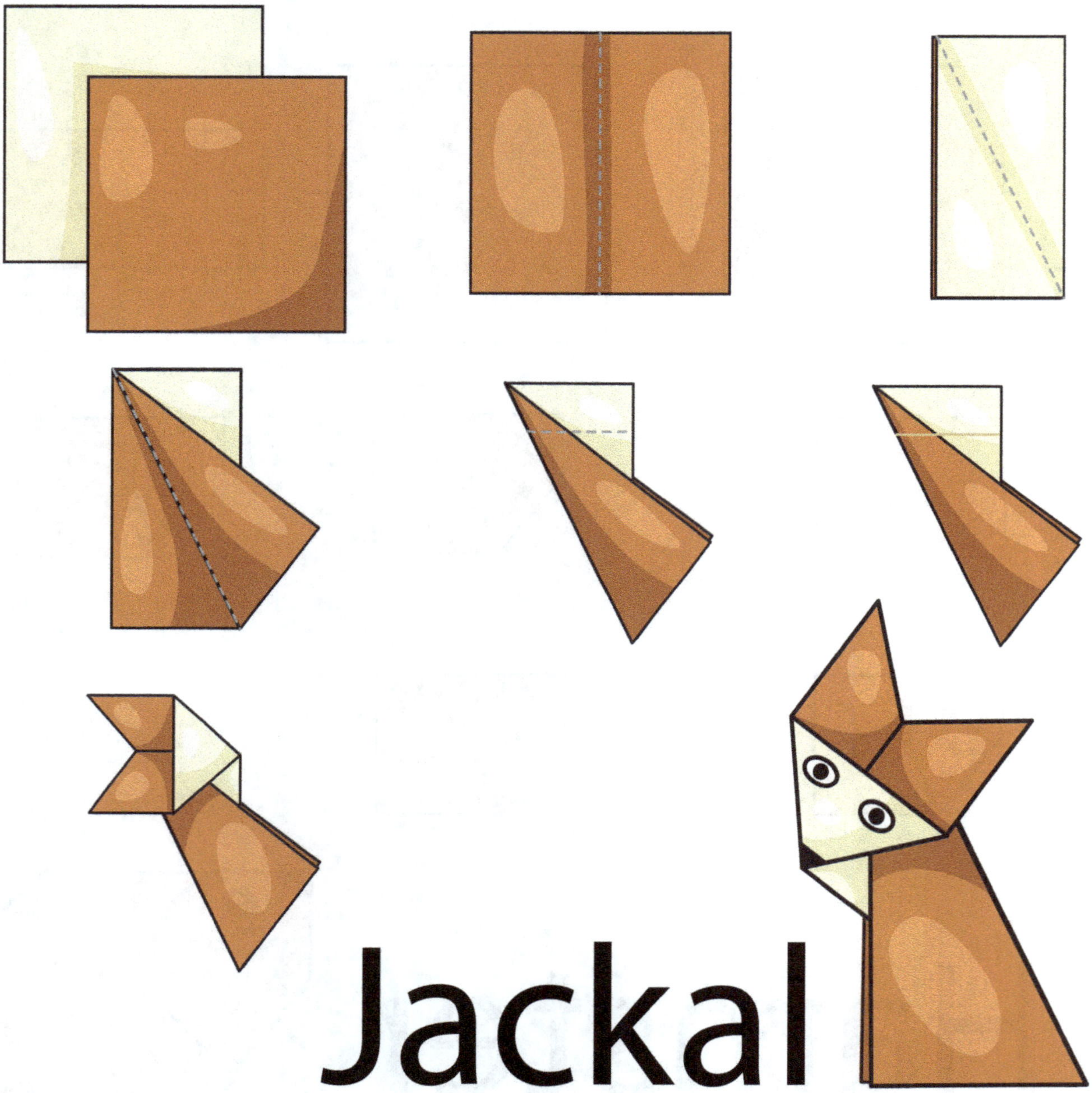

Jackal

Koala

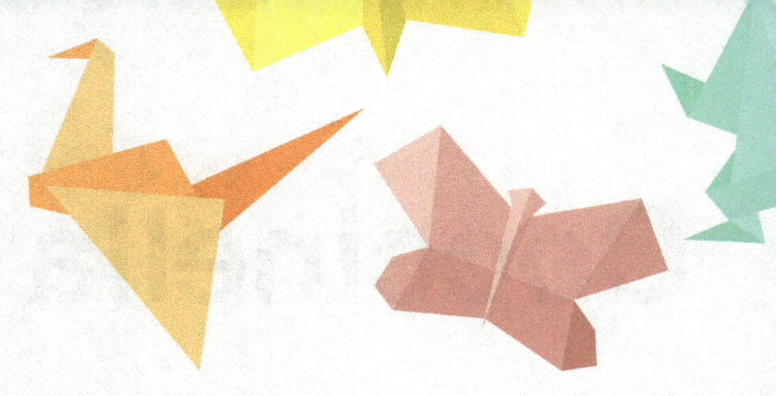

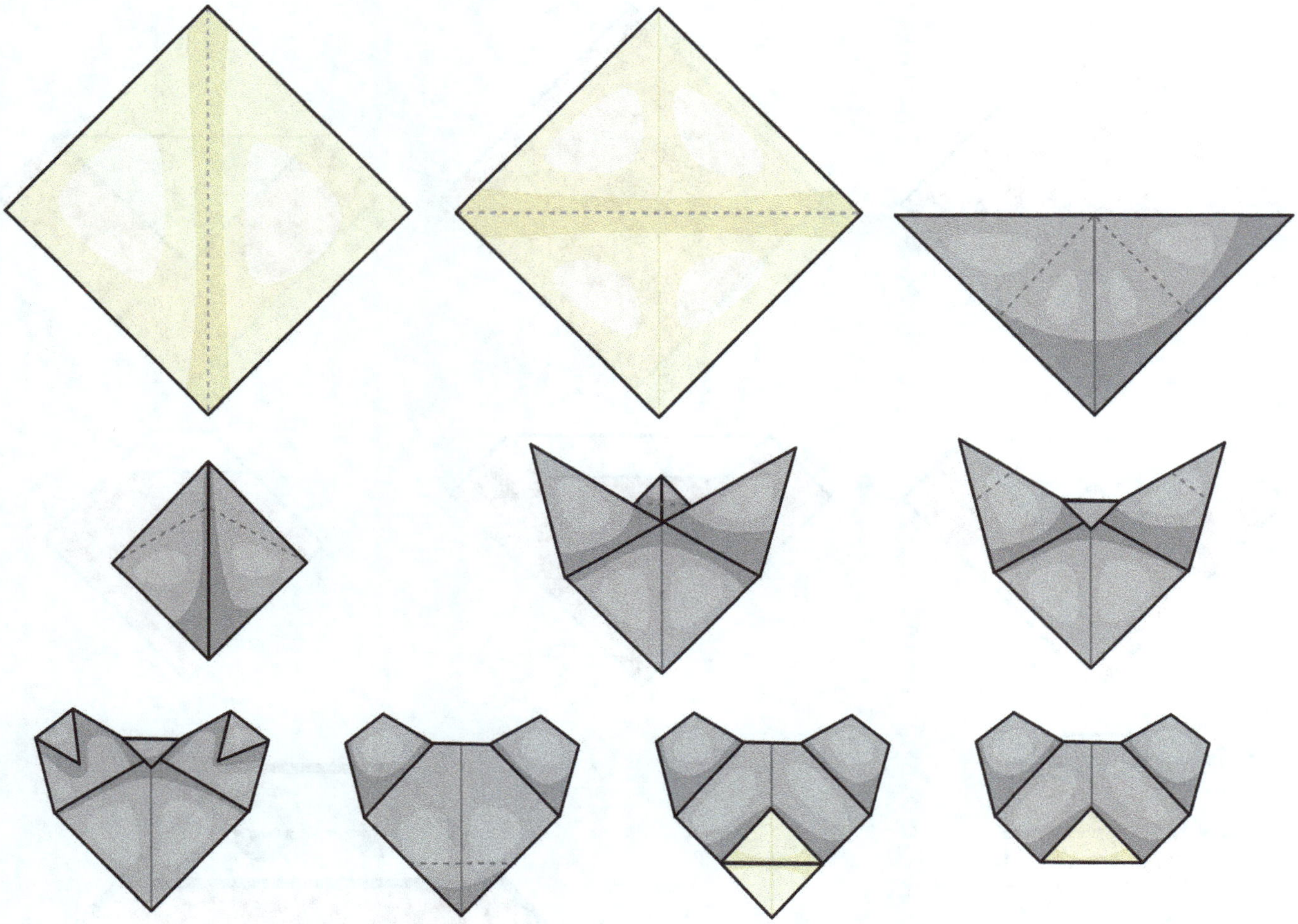

Koala

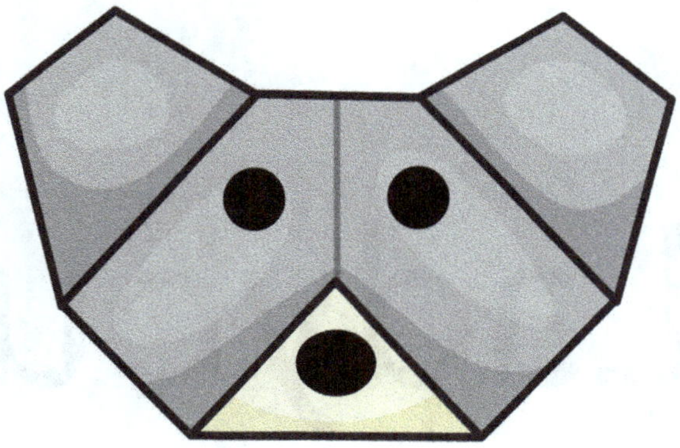

Coccinella

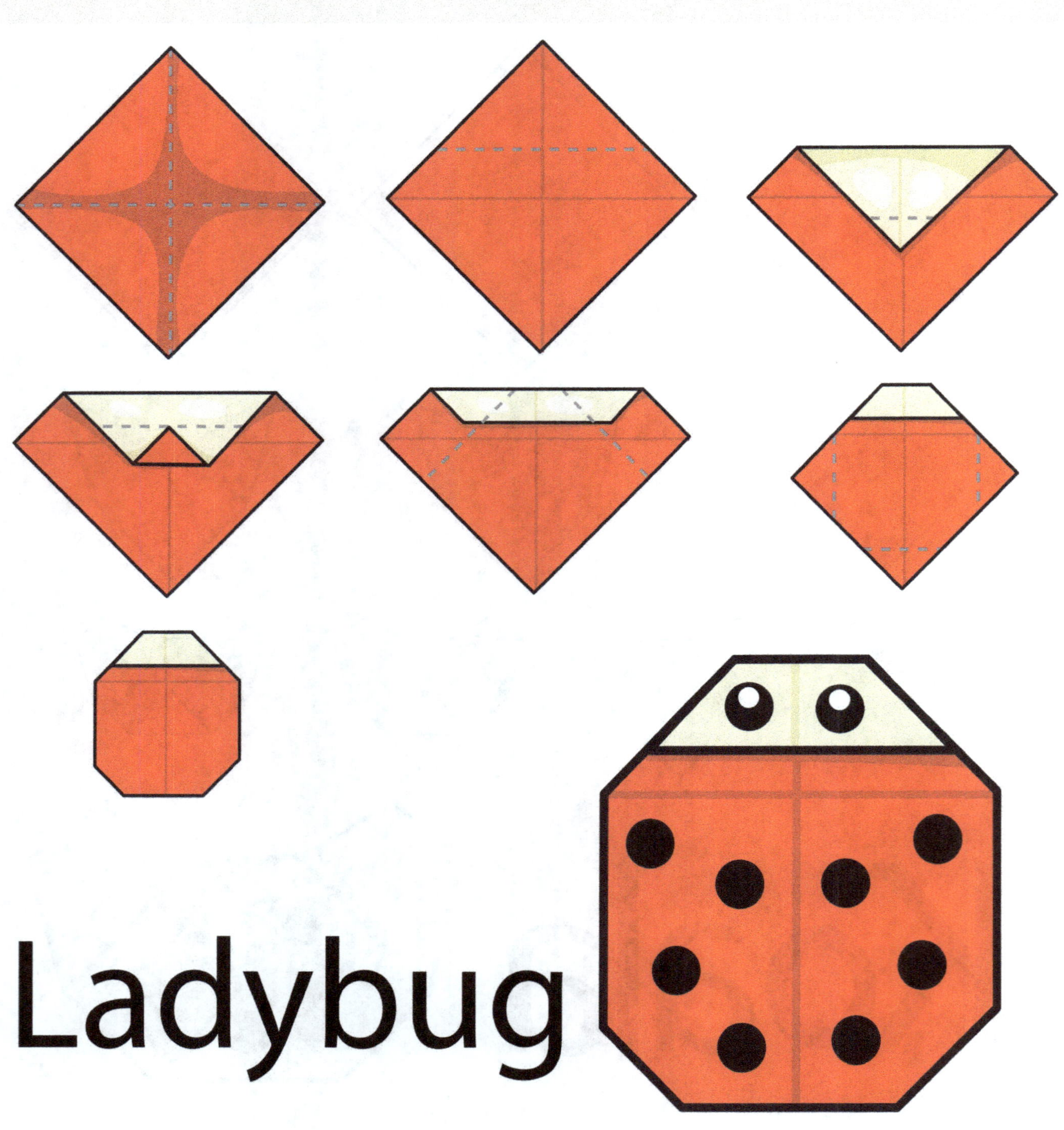

Ladybug

Scimmia

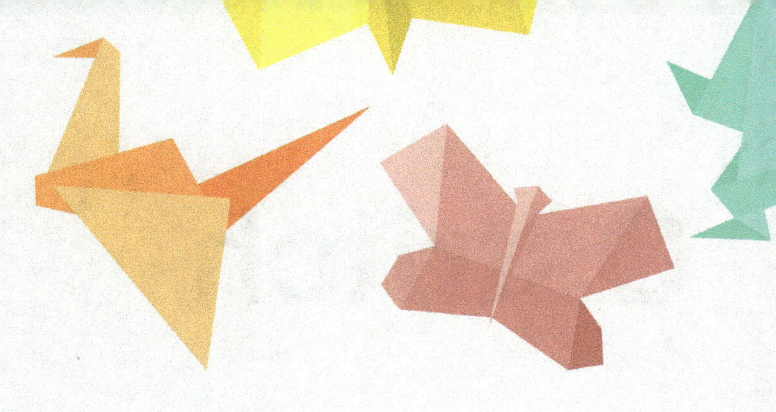

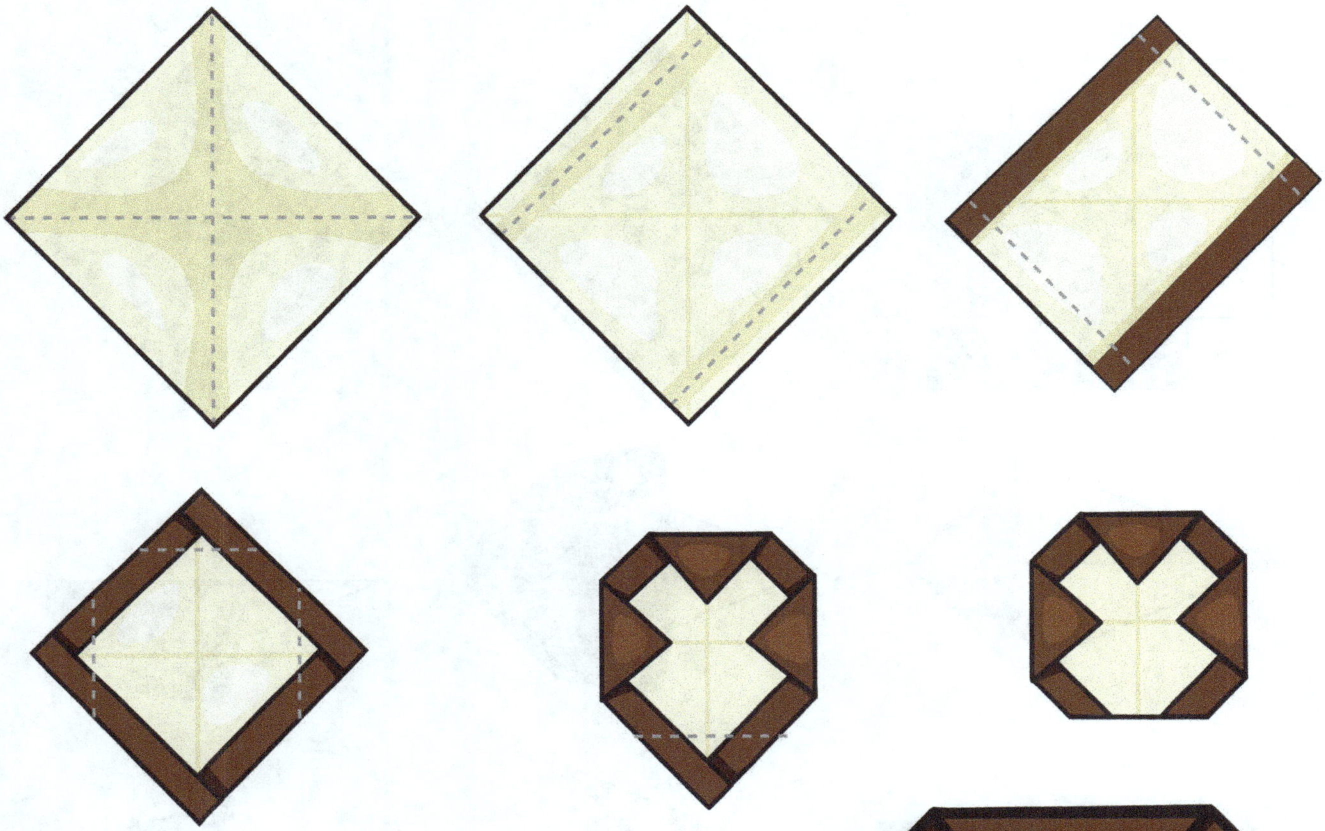

Monkey

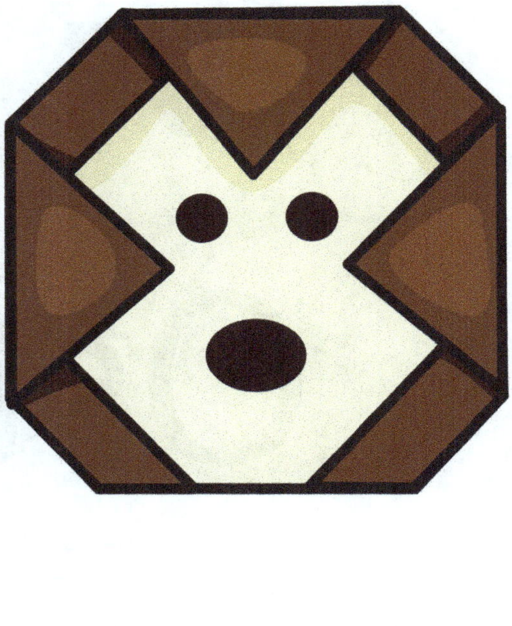

Ostritch

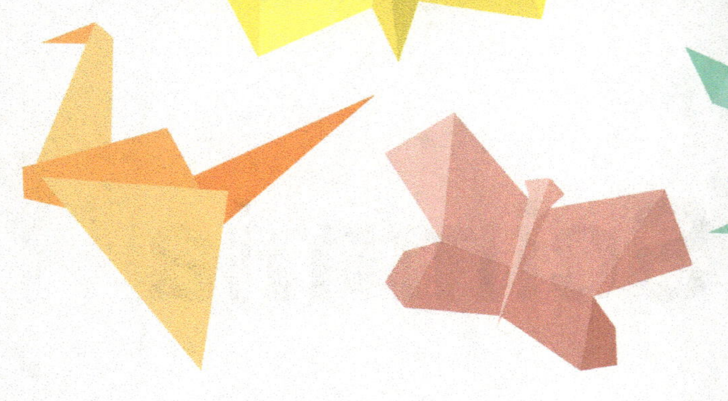

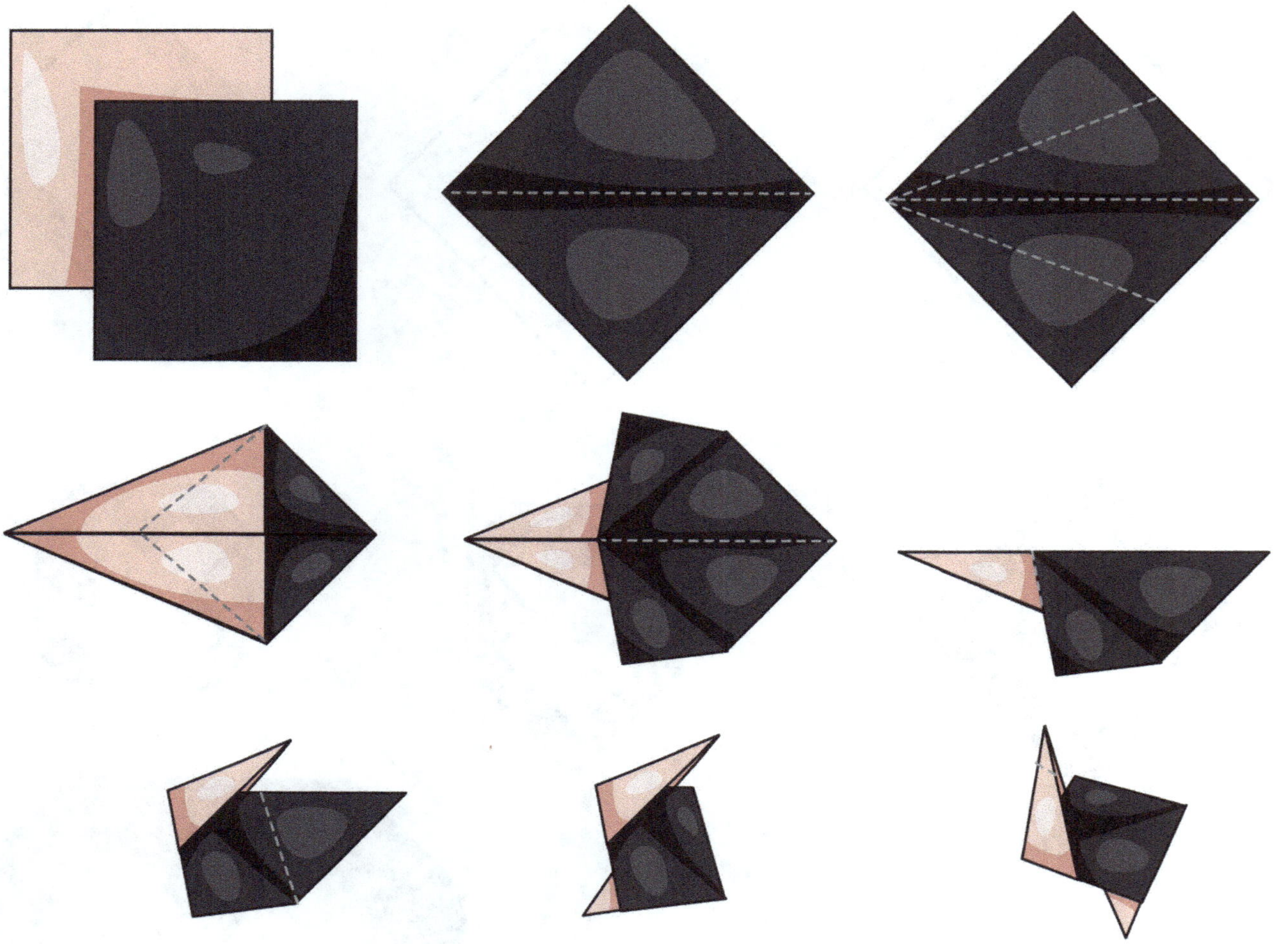

Ostrich

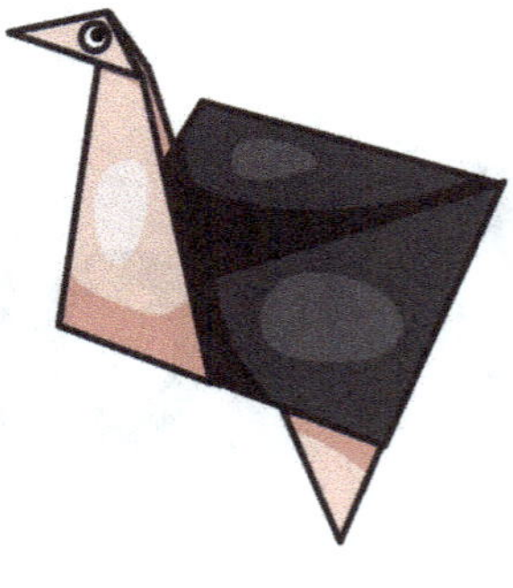

Panda

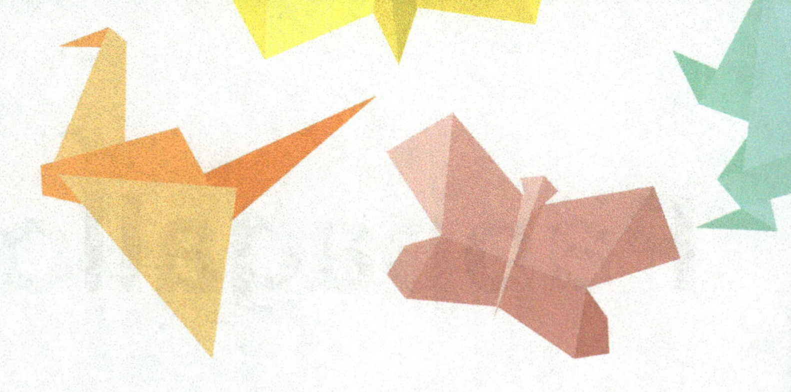

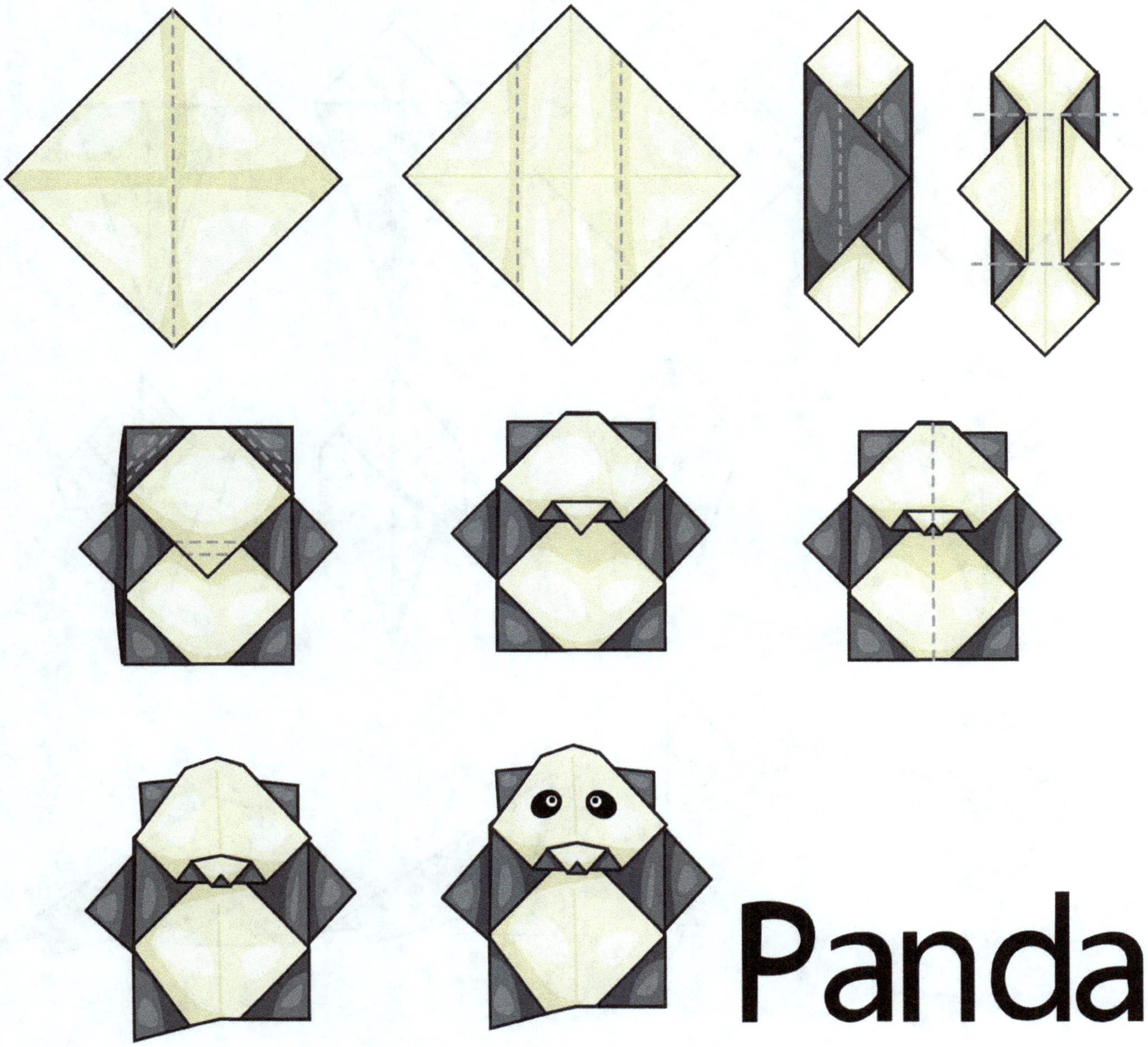

Panda

Pappagallo

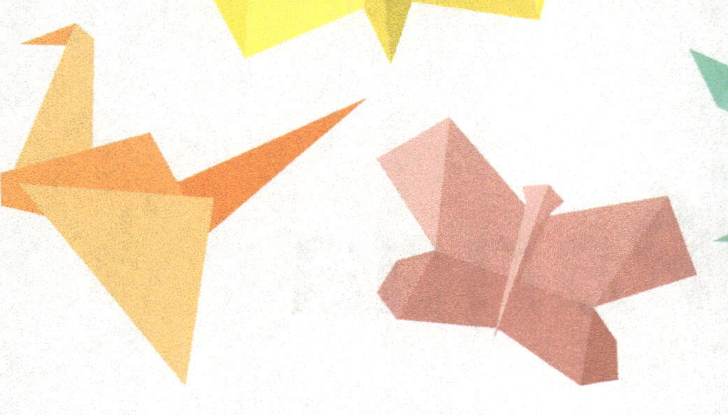

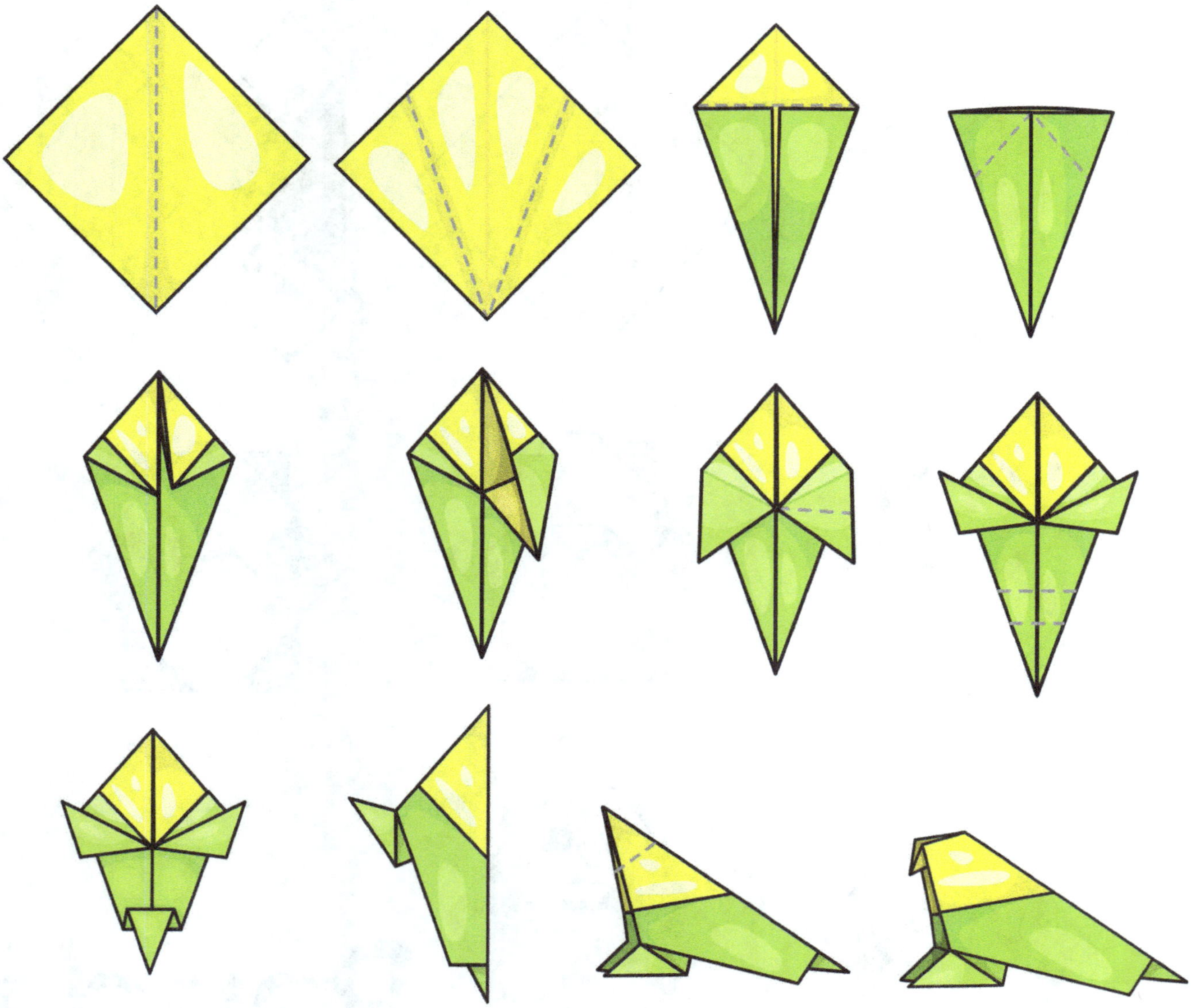

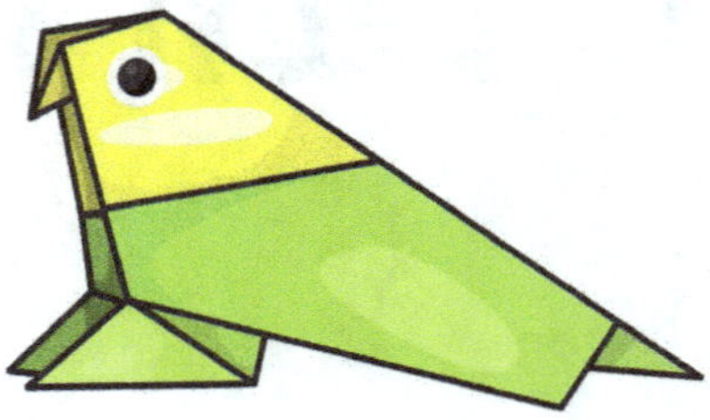

Parrot

Pavone

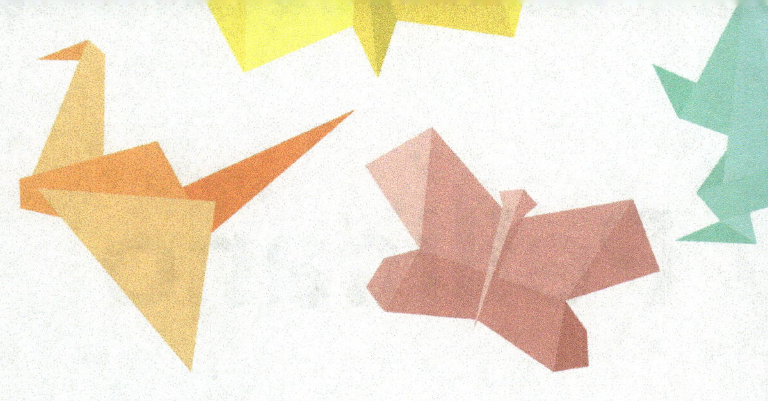

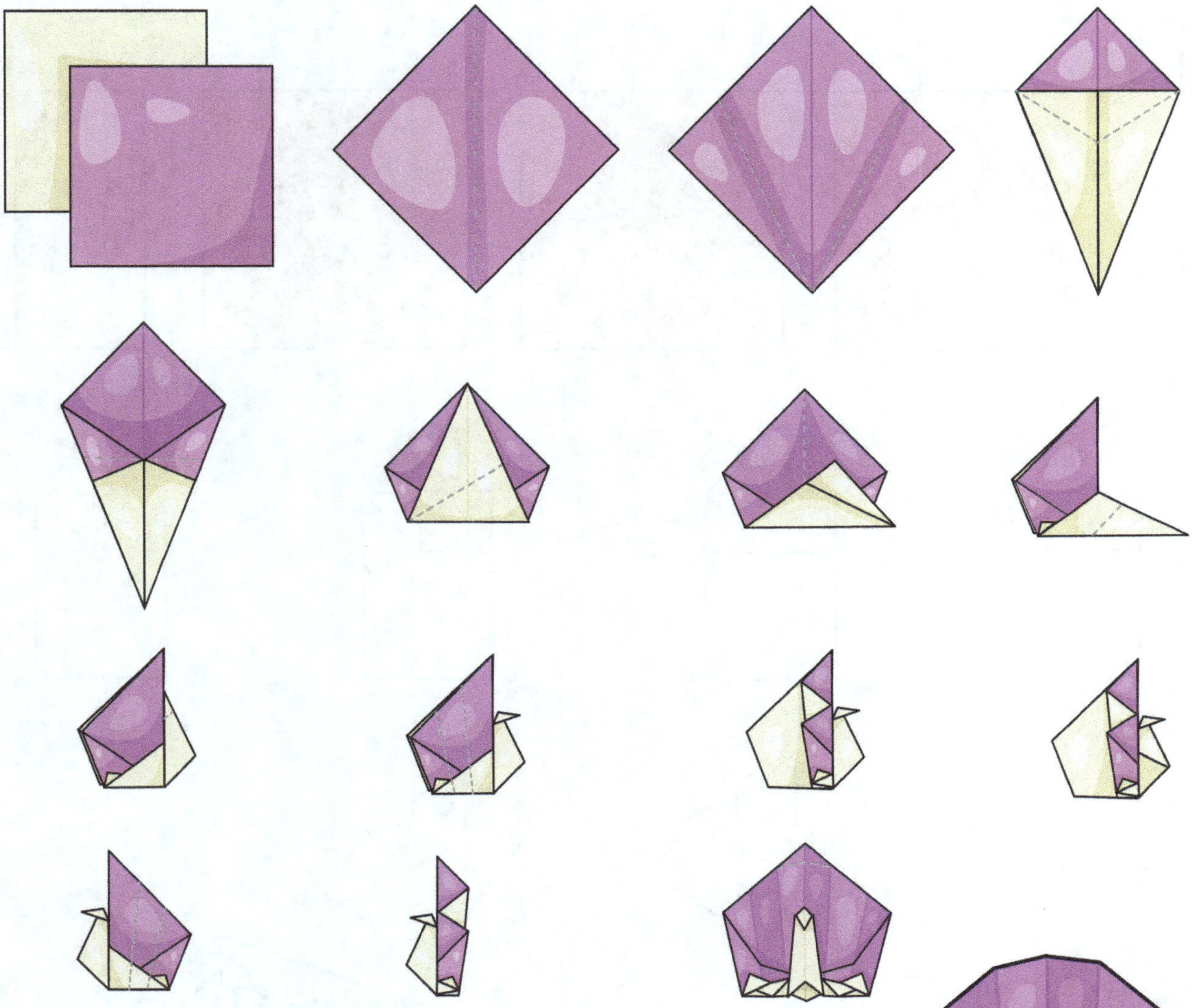

Peacock

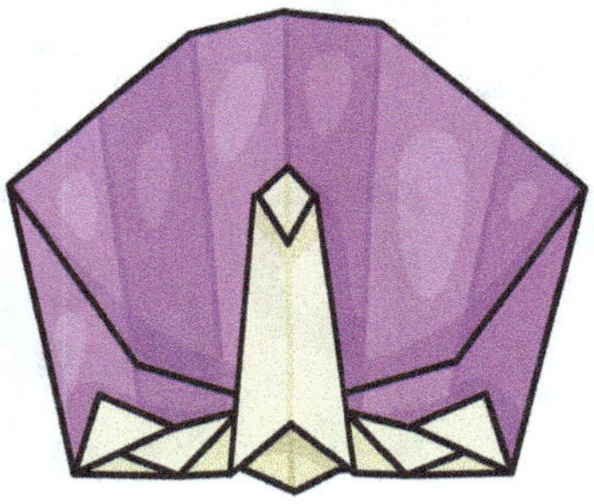

Pellicano

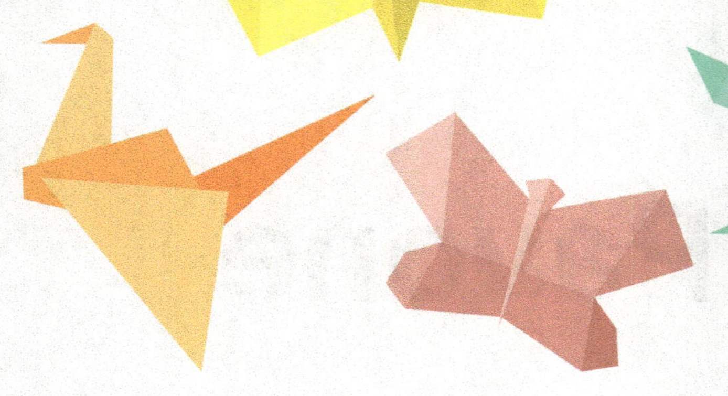

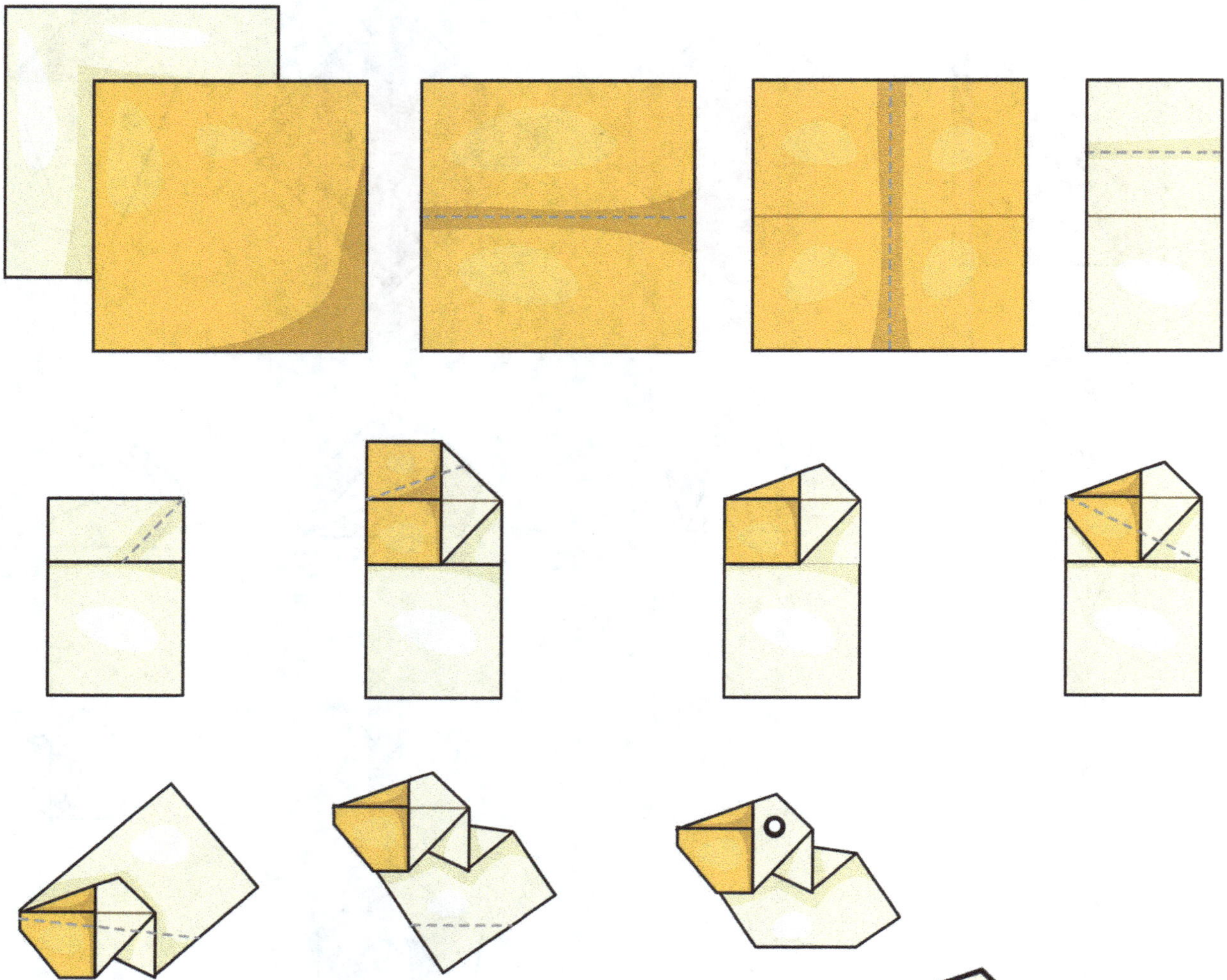

Pelican

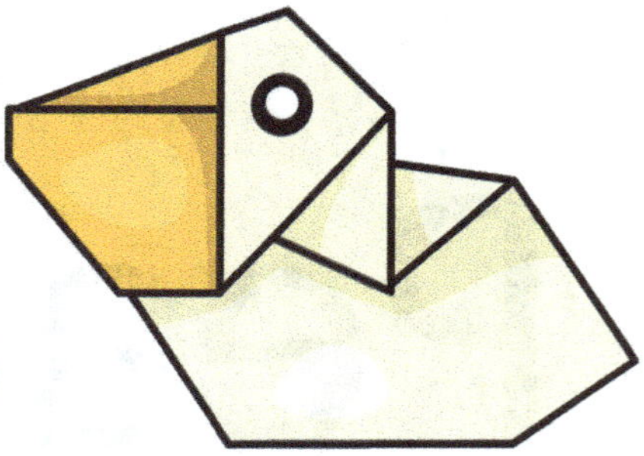

Pinguino

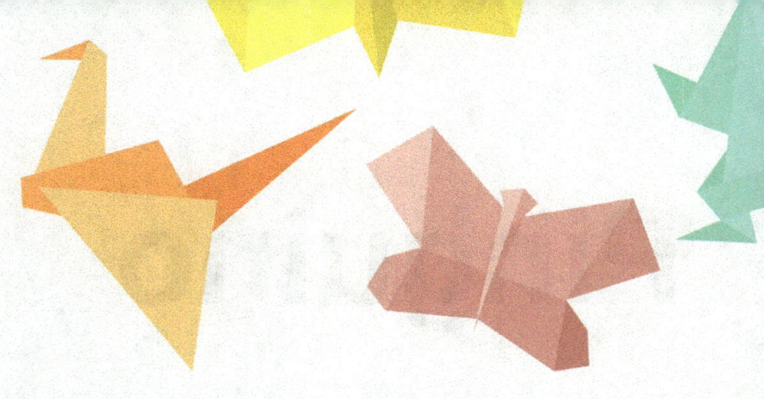

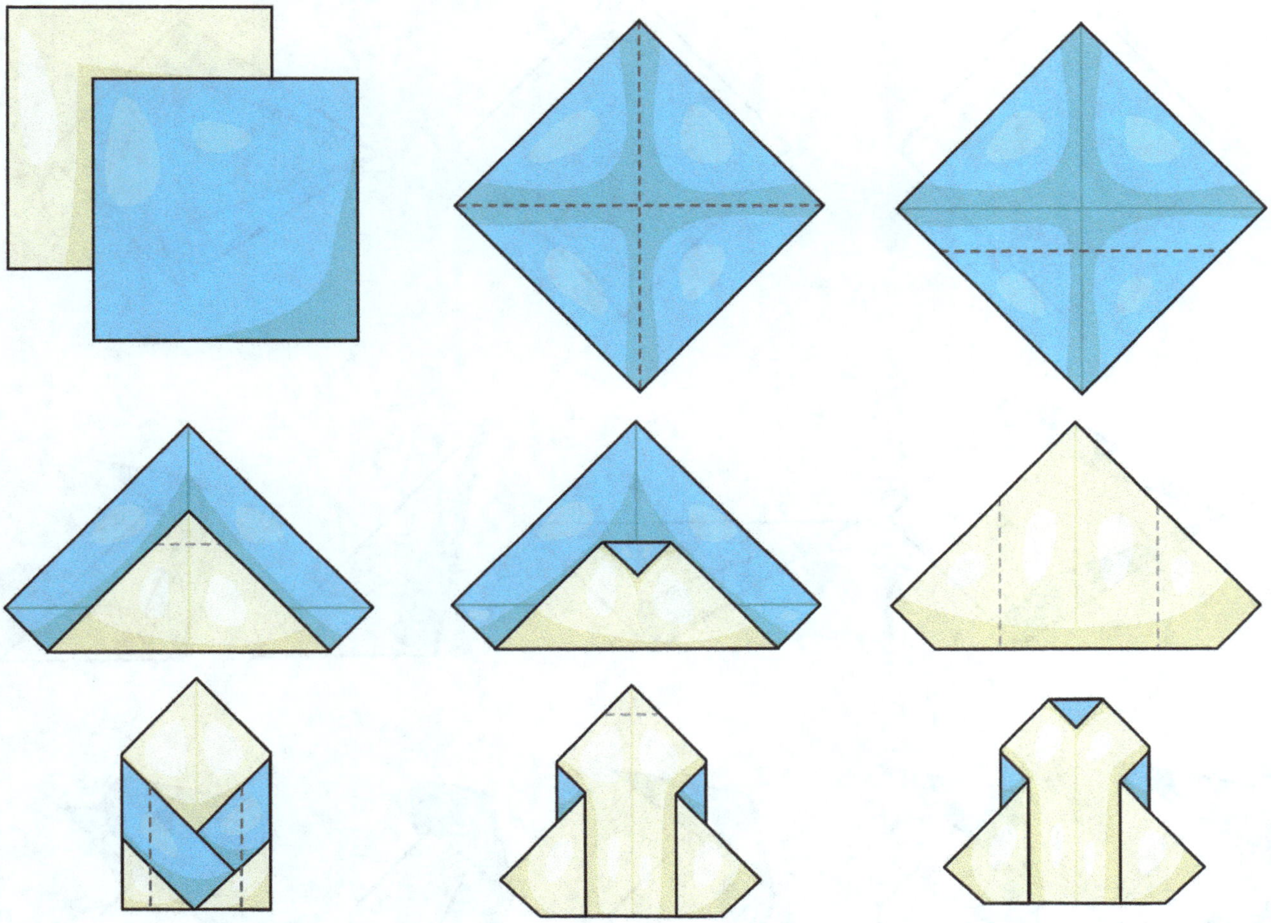

Penguin

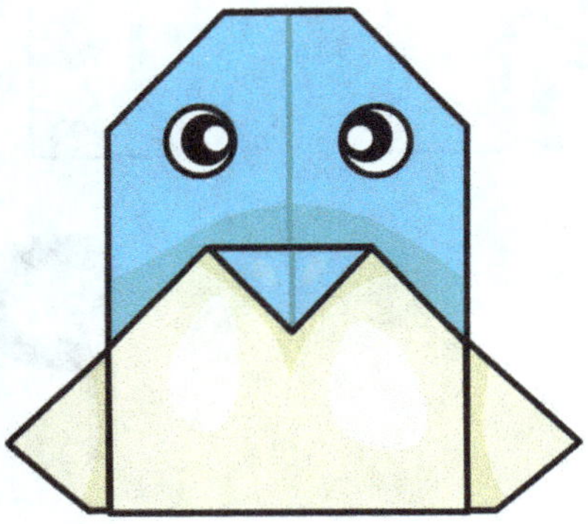

Pinguino

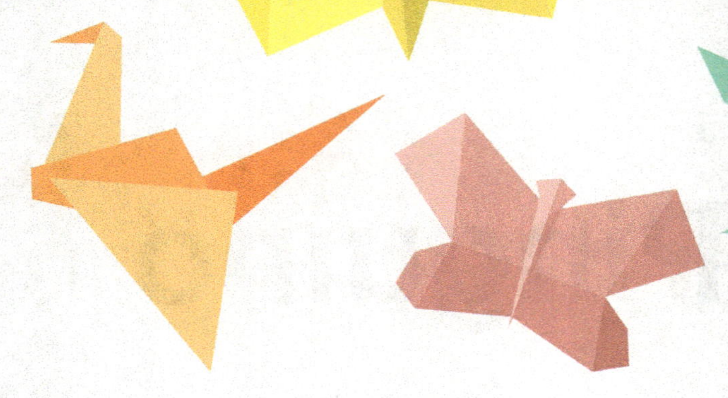

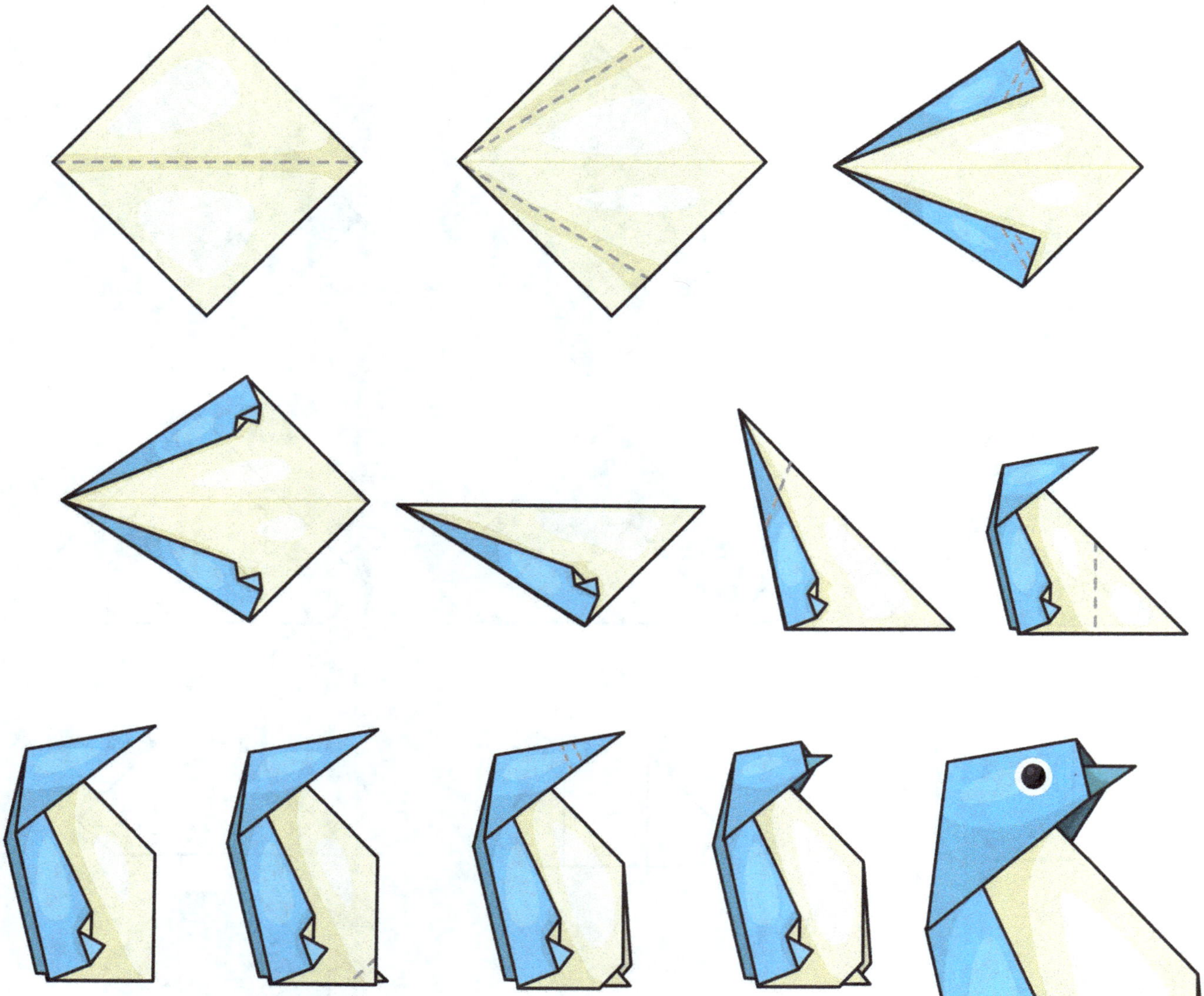

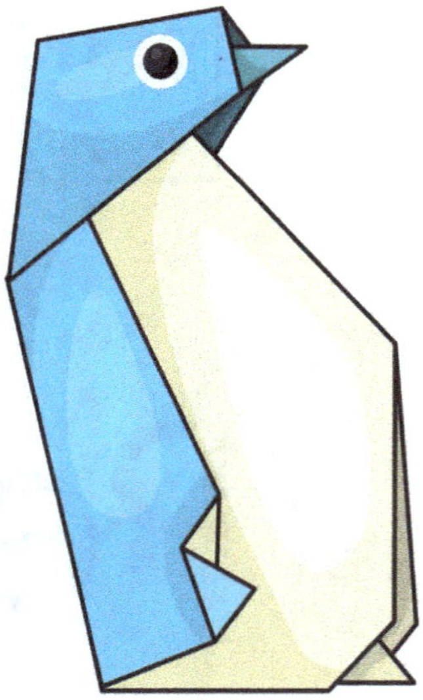

Penguin

Maiale

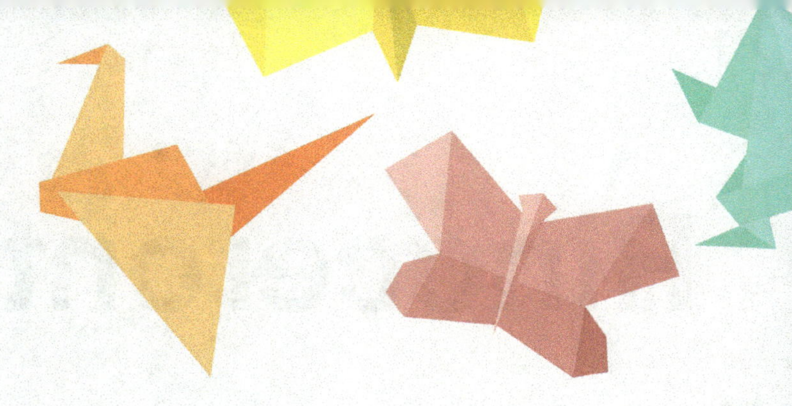

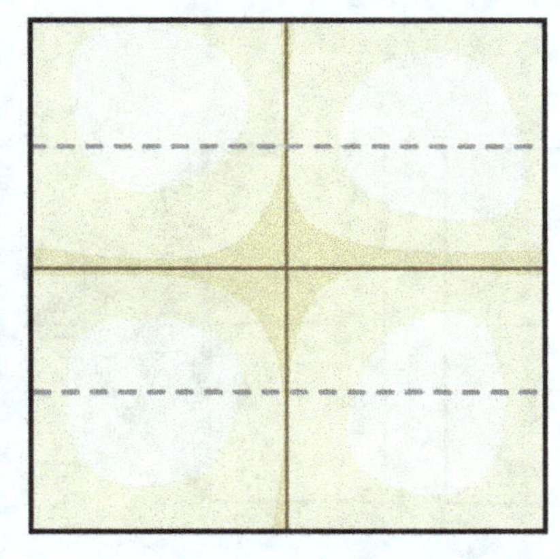

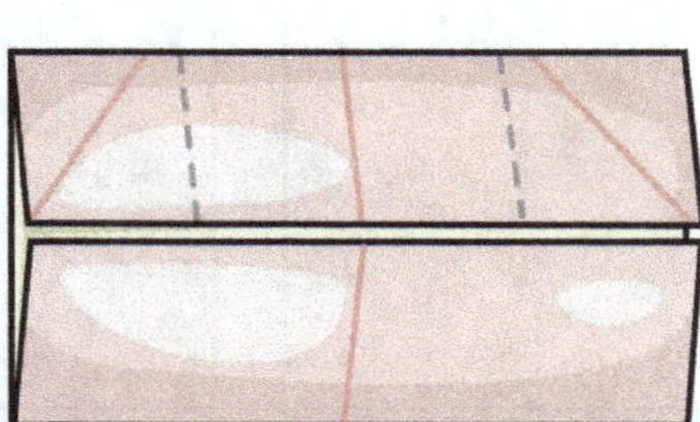

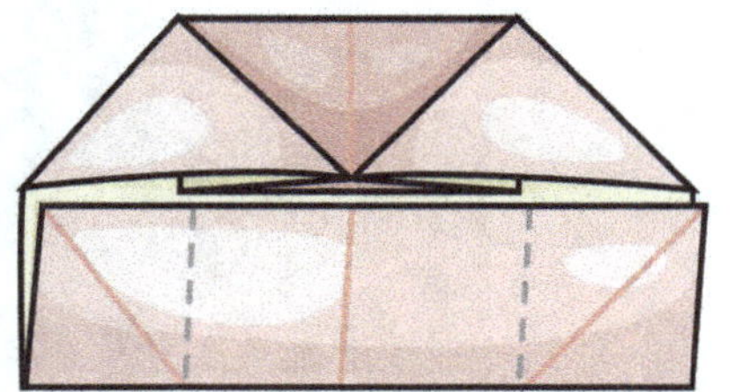

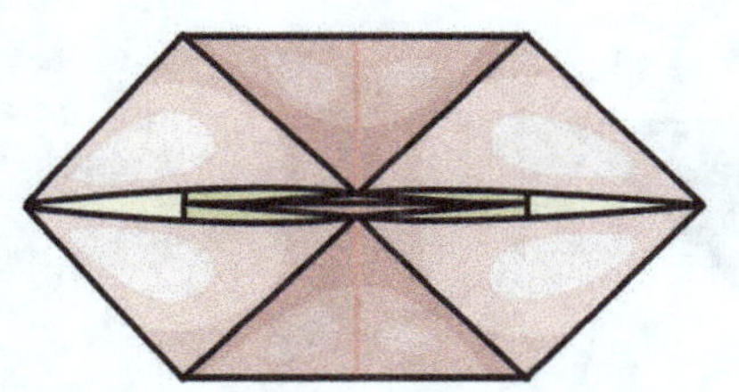

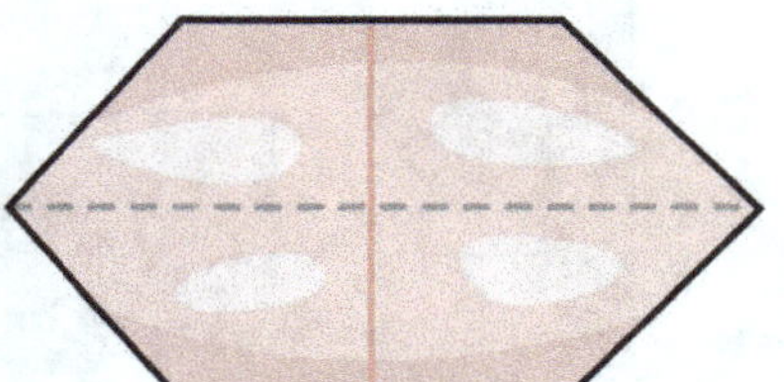

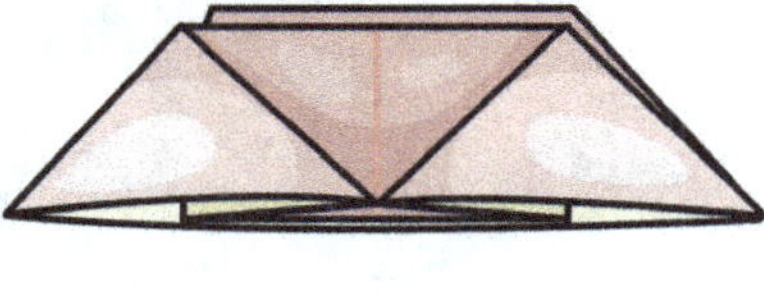

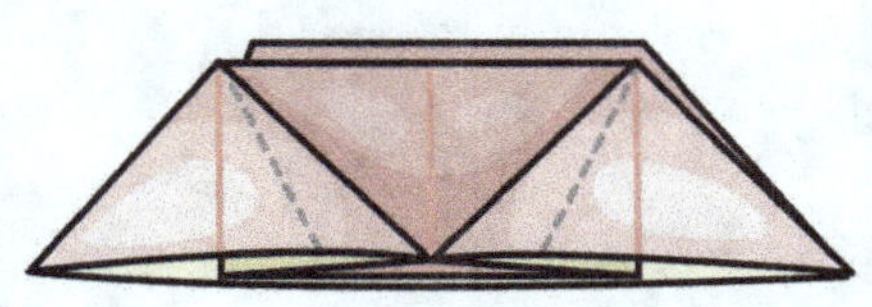

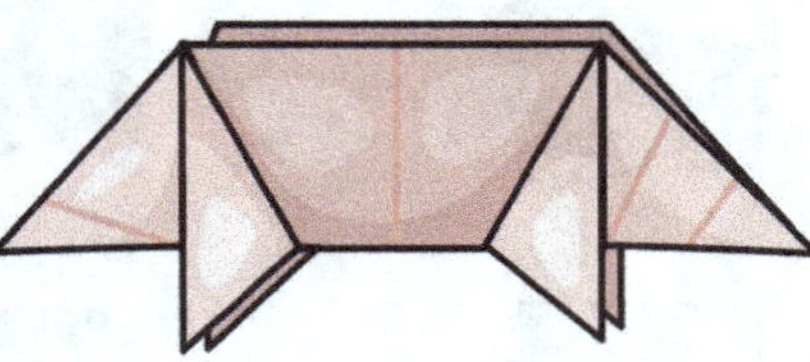

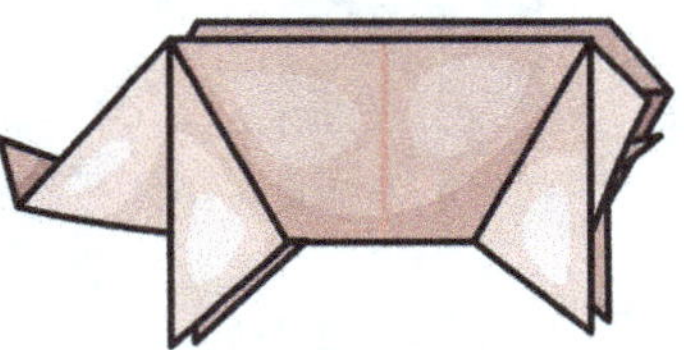

Pig

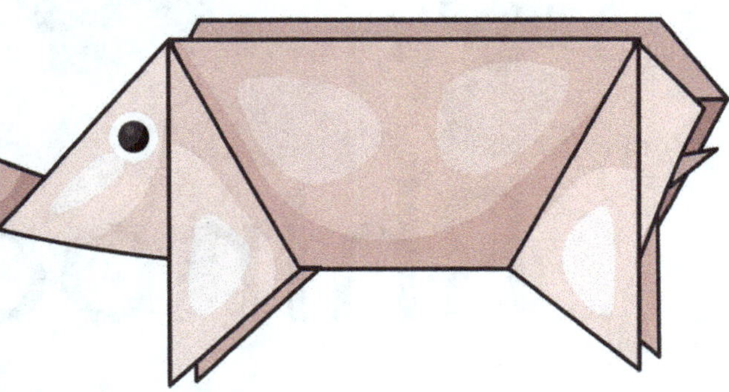

Rinoceronte

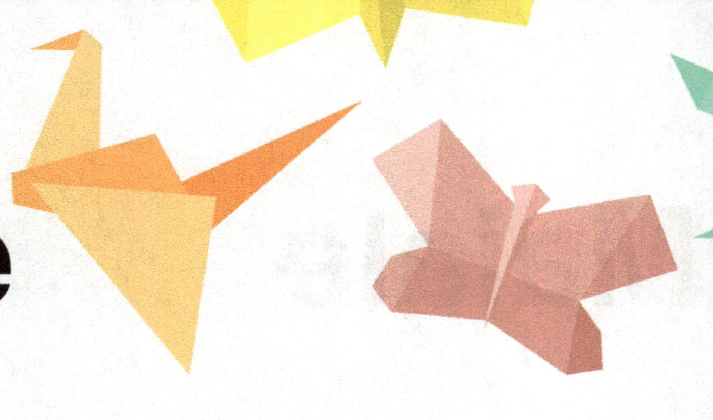

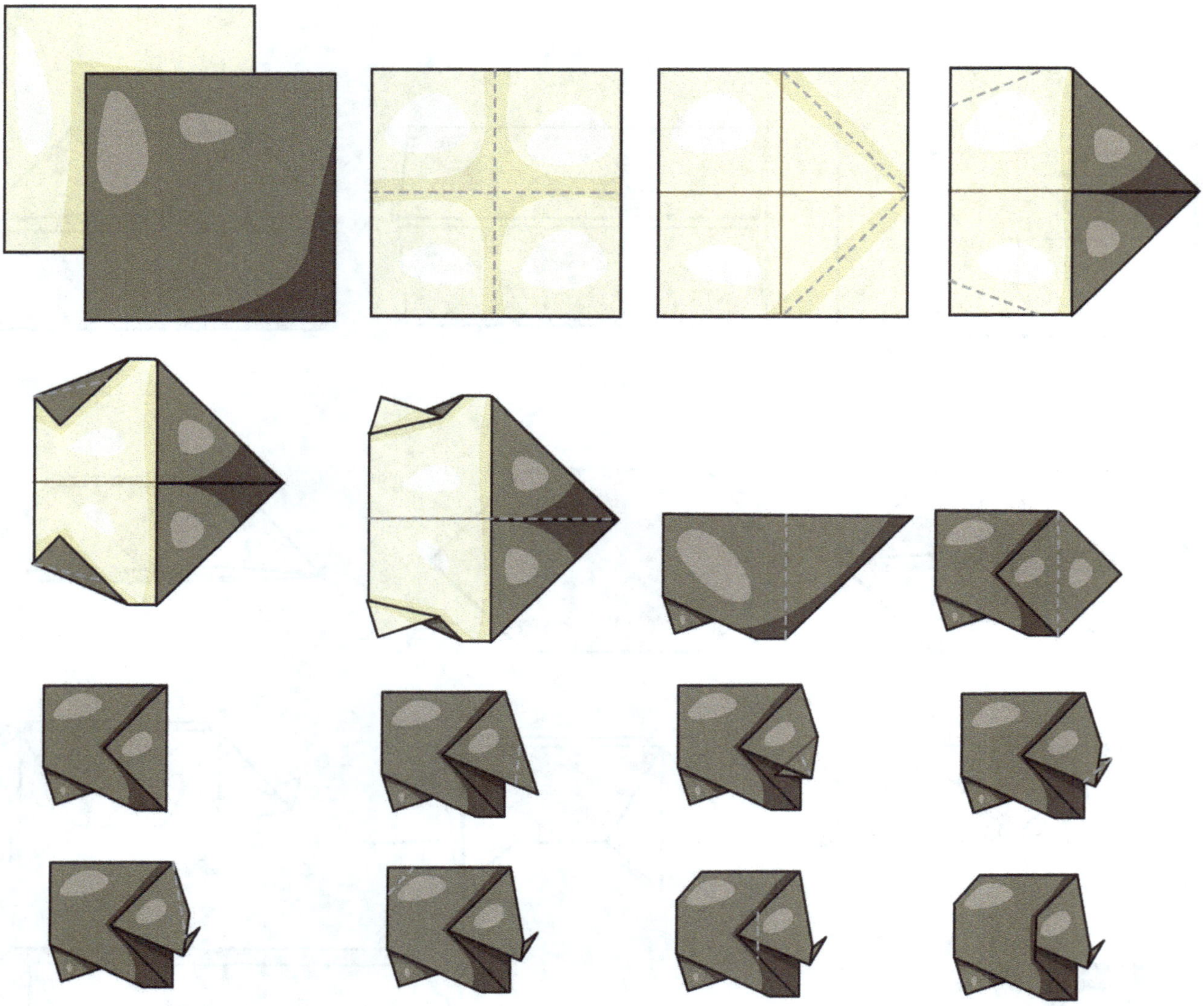

Rhinoceros

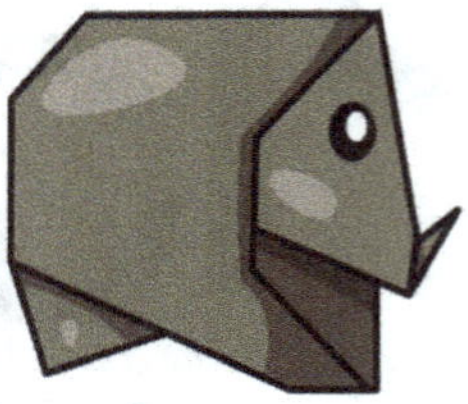

Nave

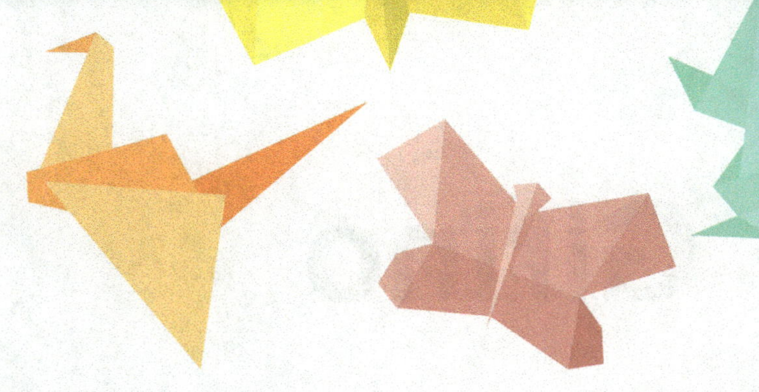

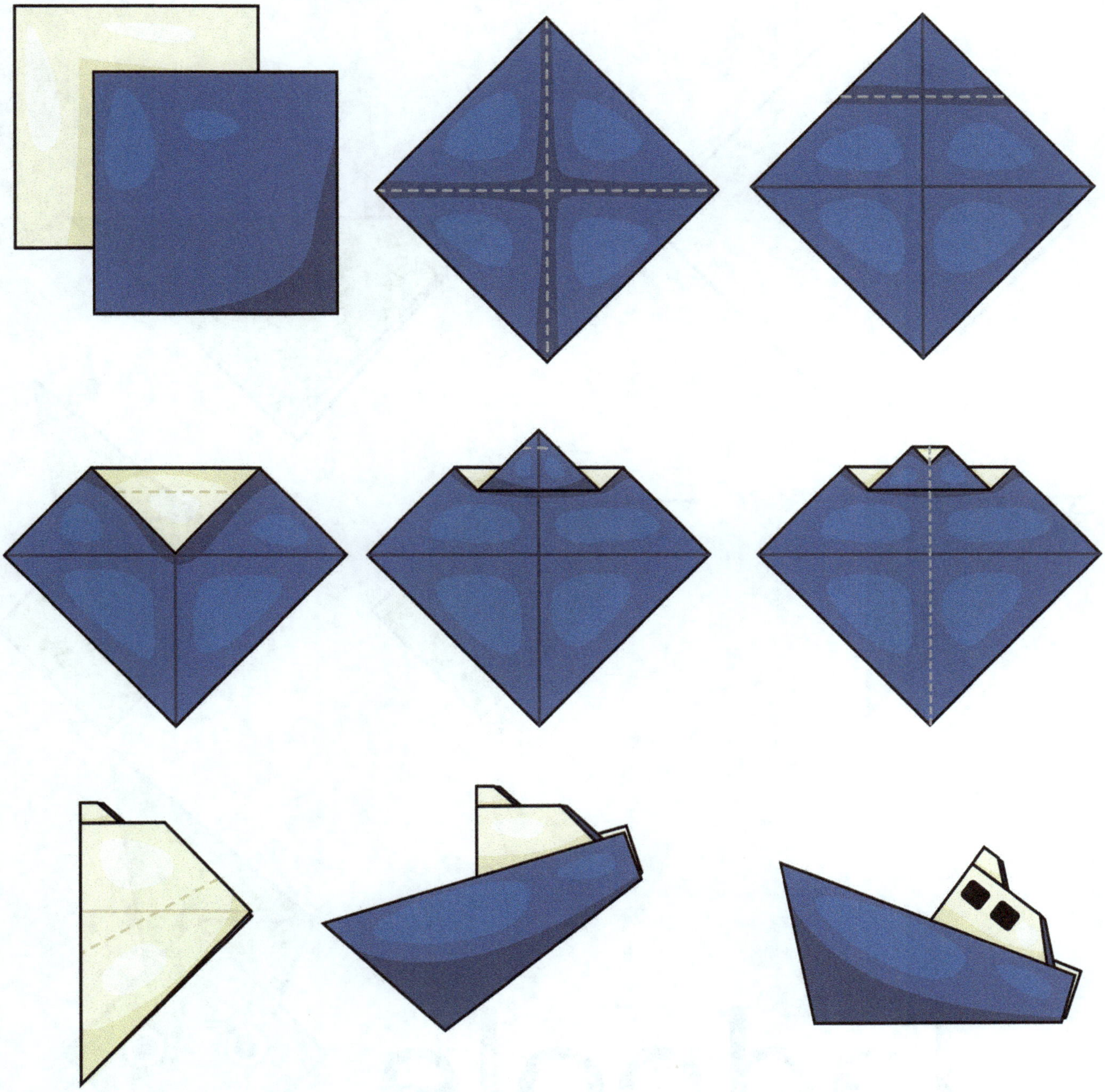

Girino

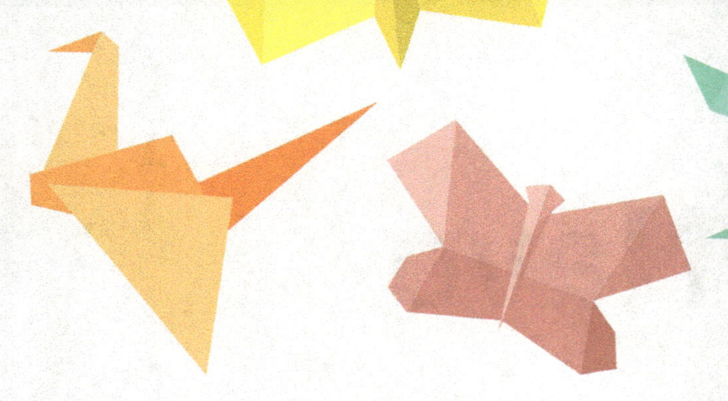

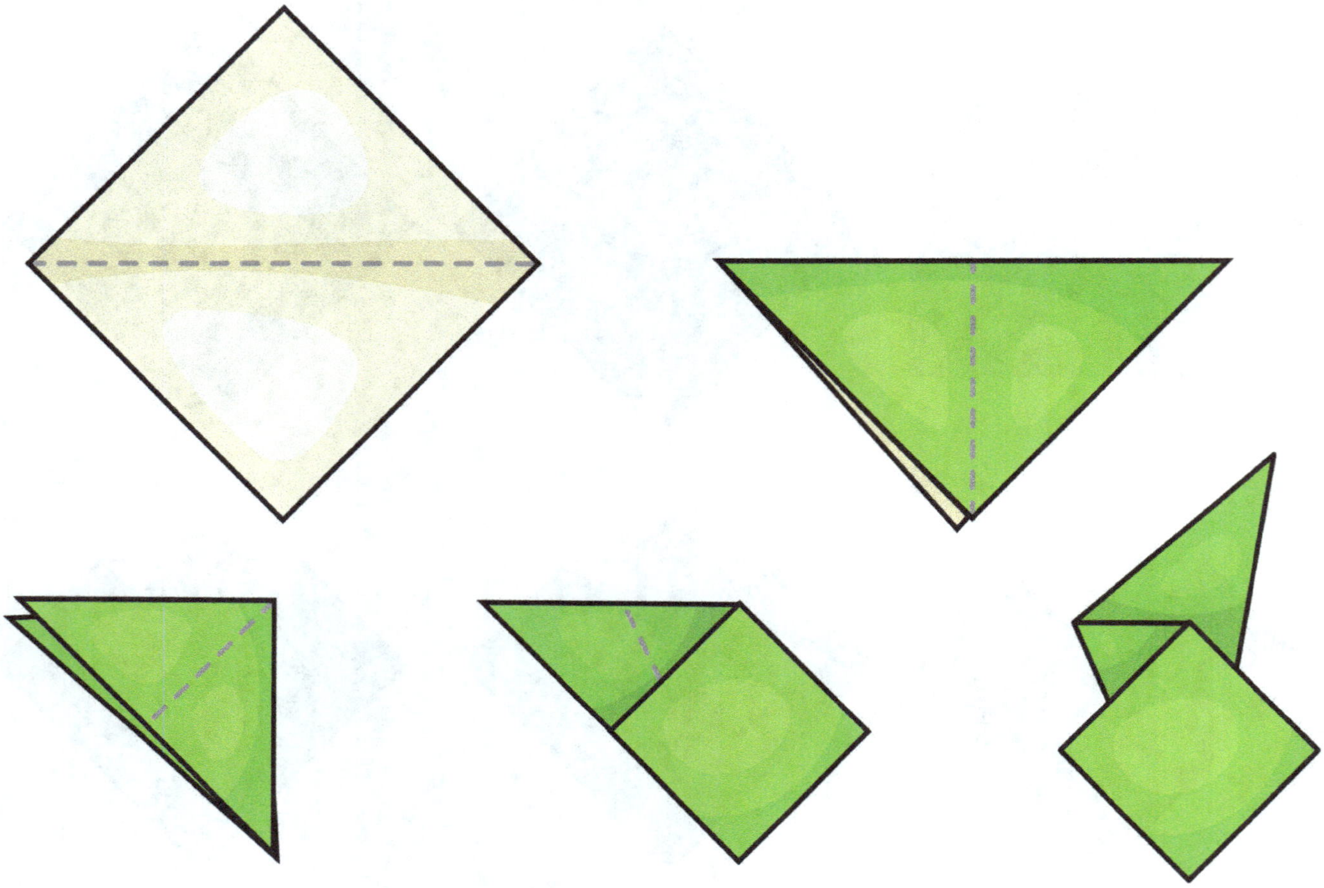

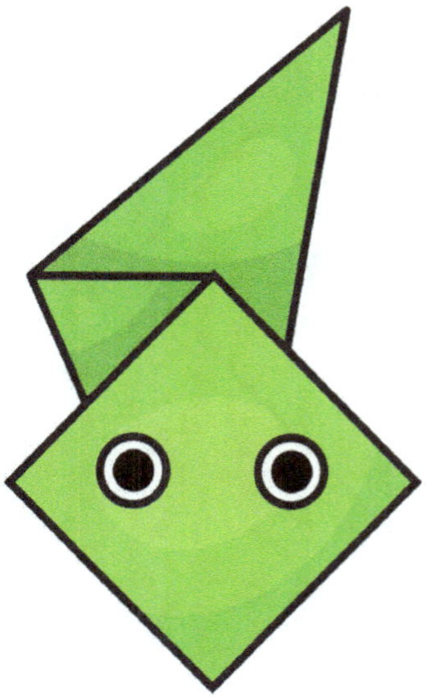

Tadpole

Tartaruga

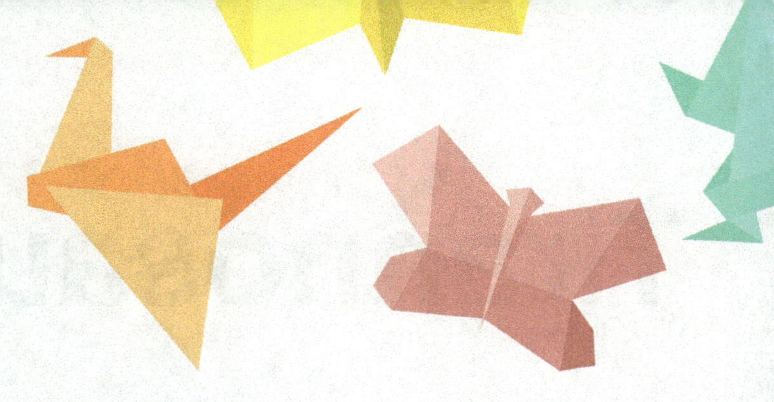

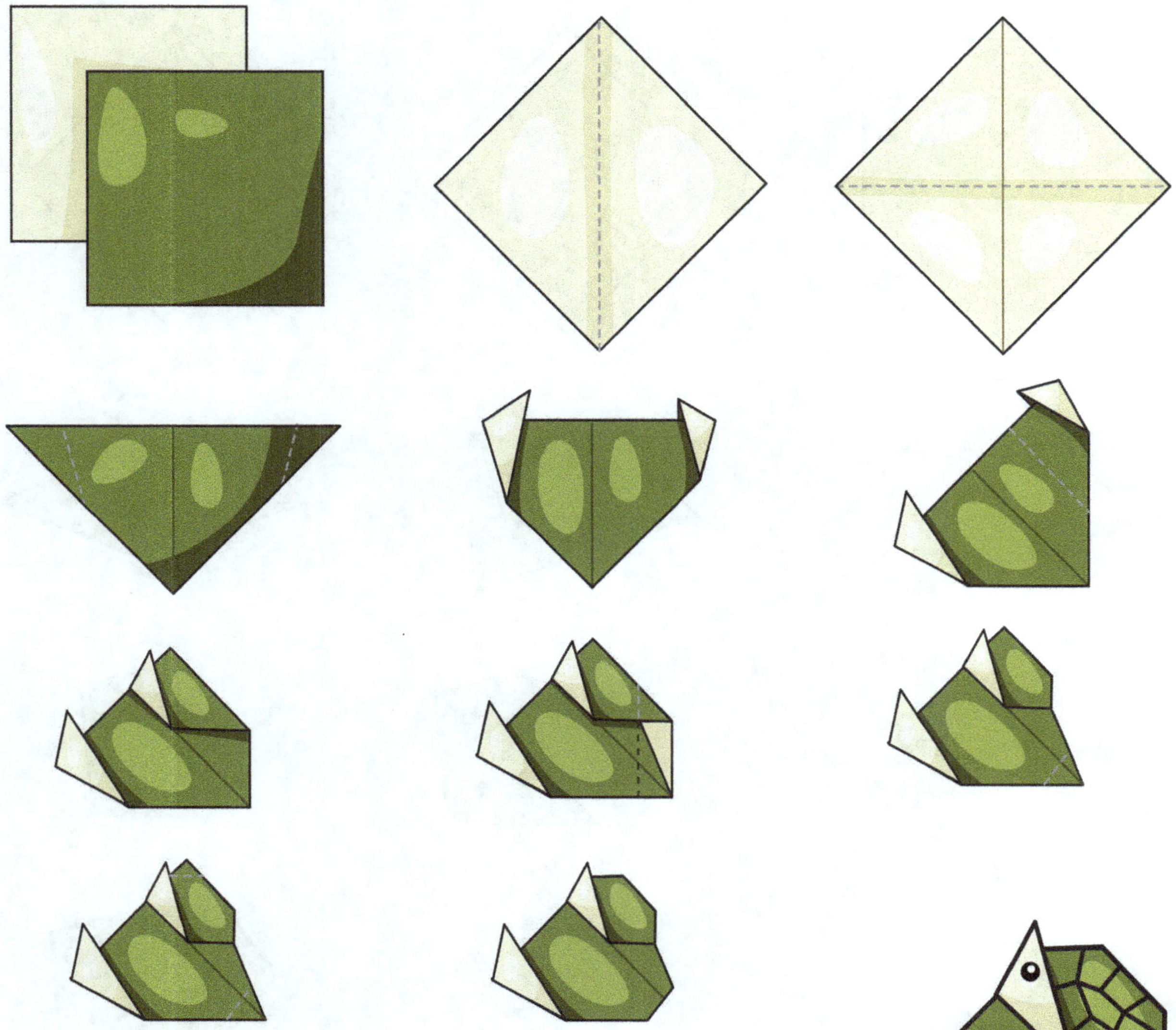

Turtle family

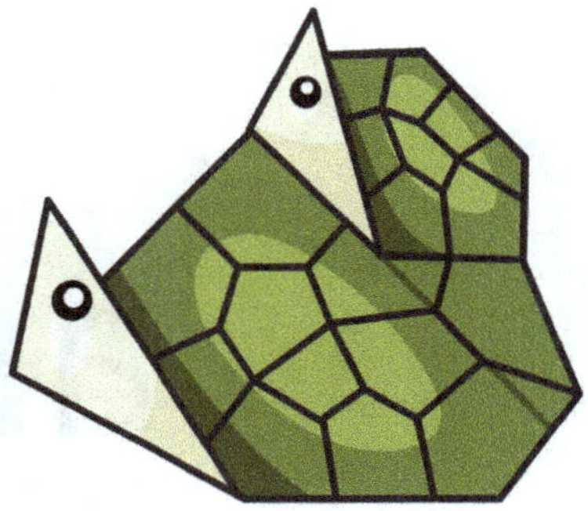

Tirannosauro

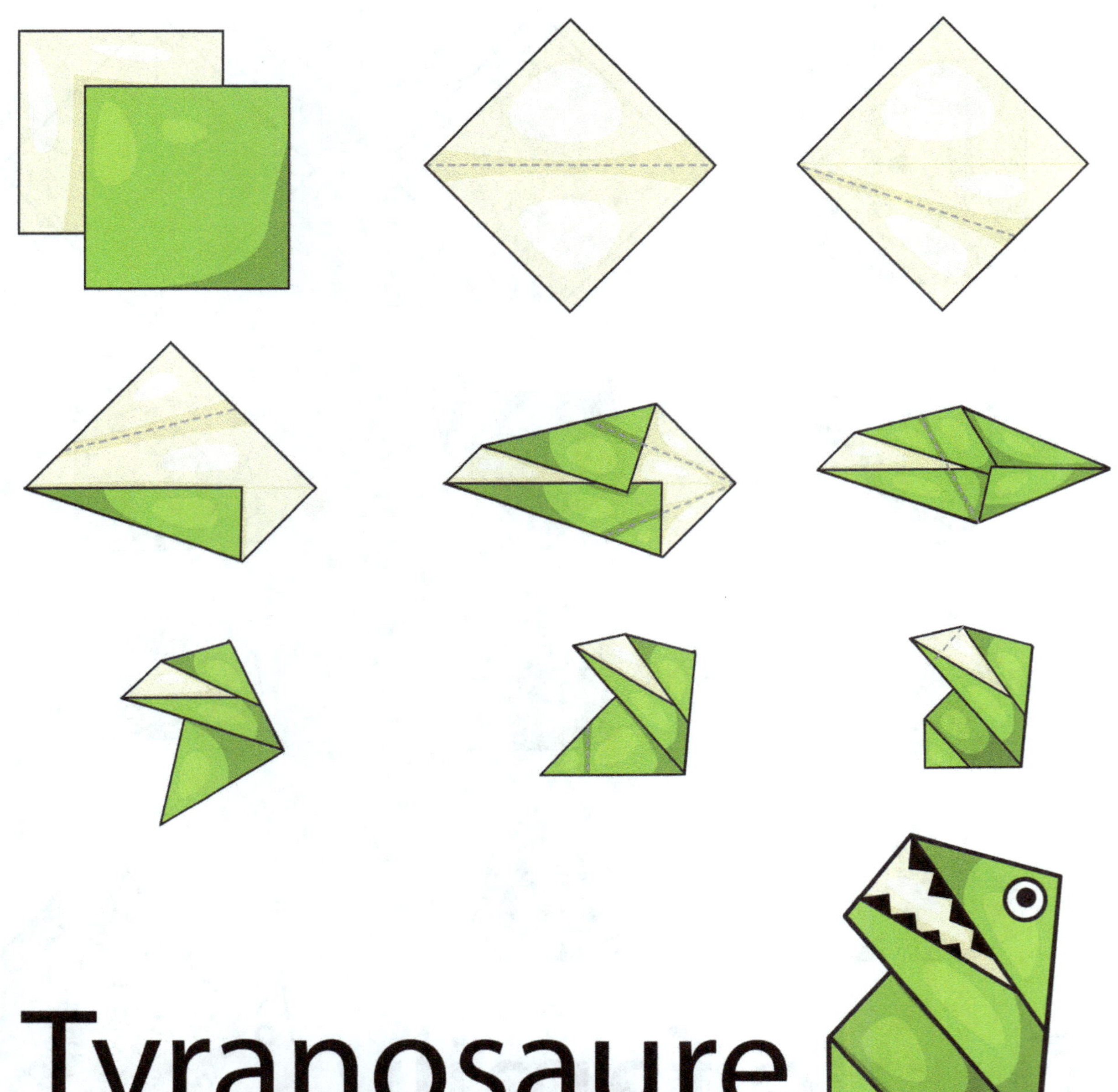

Tyranosaure

Anguria

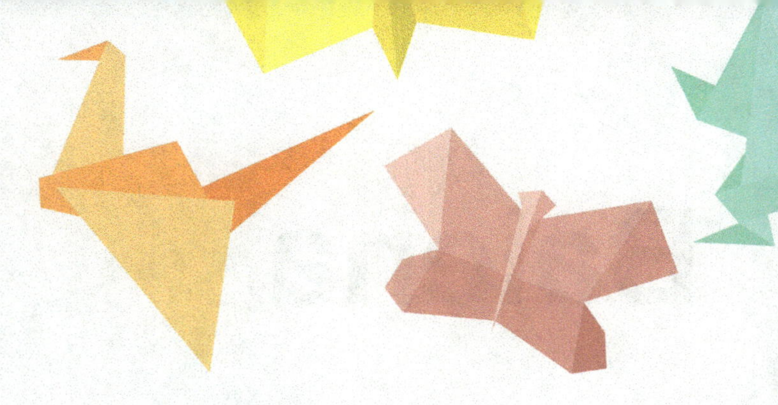

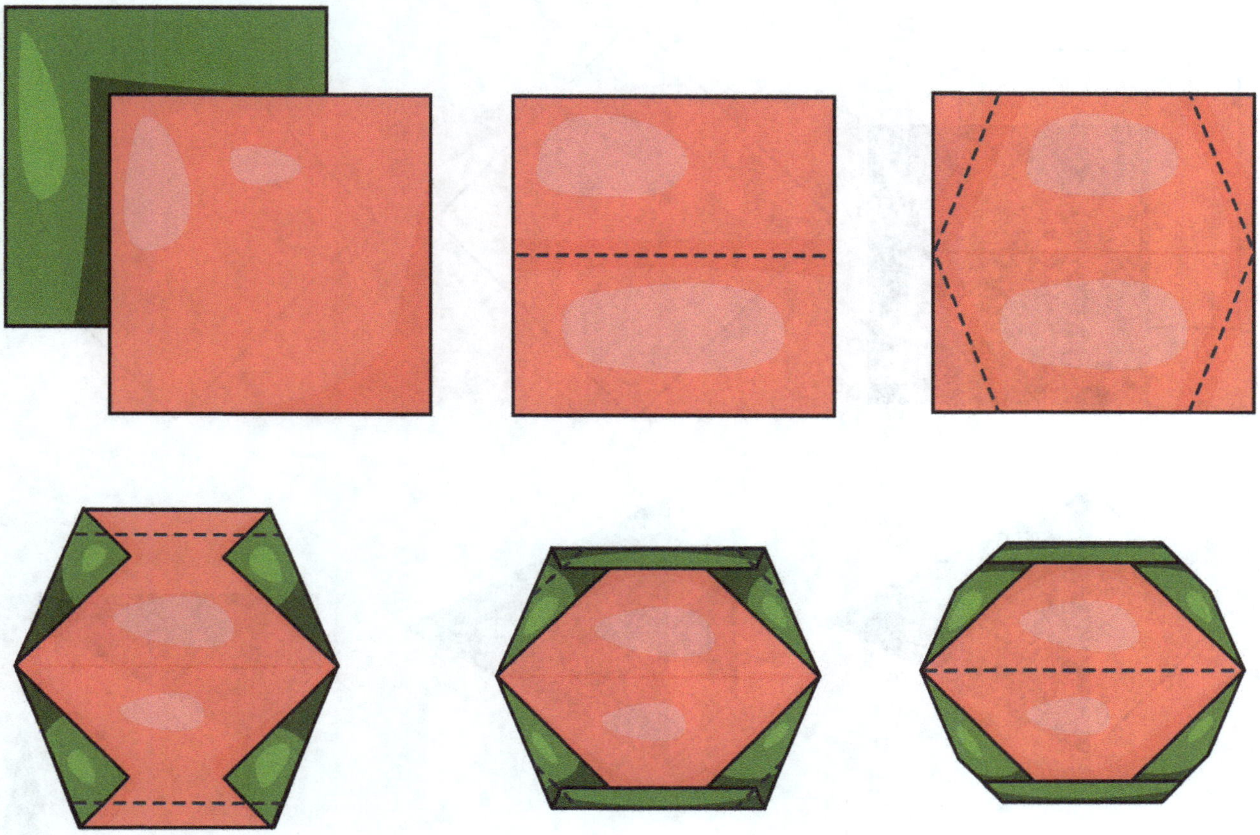

Water Melon

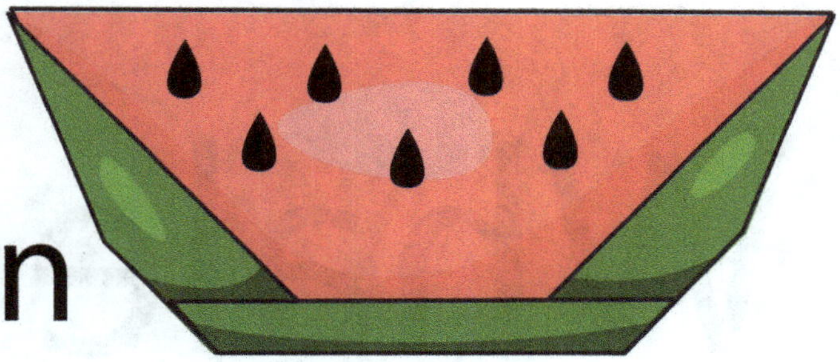

Balena

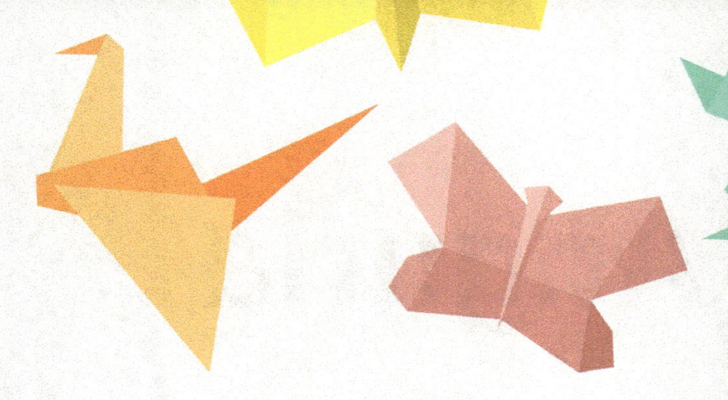

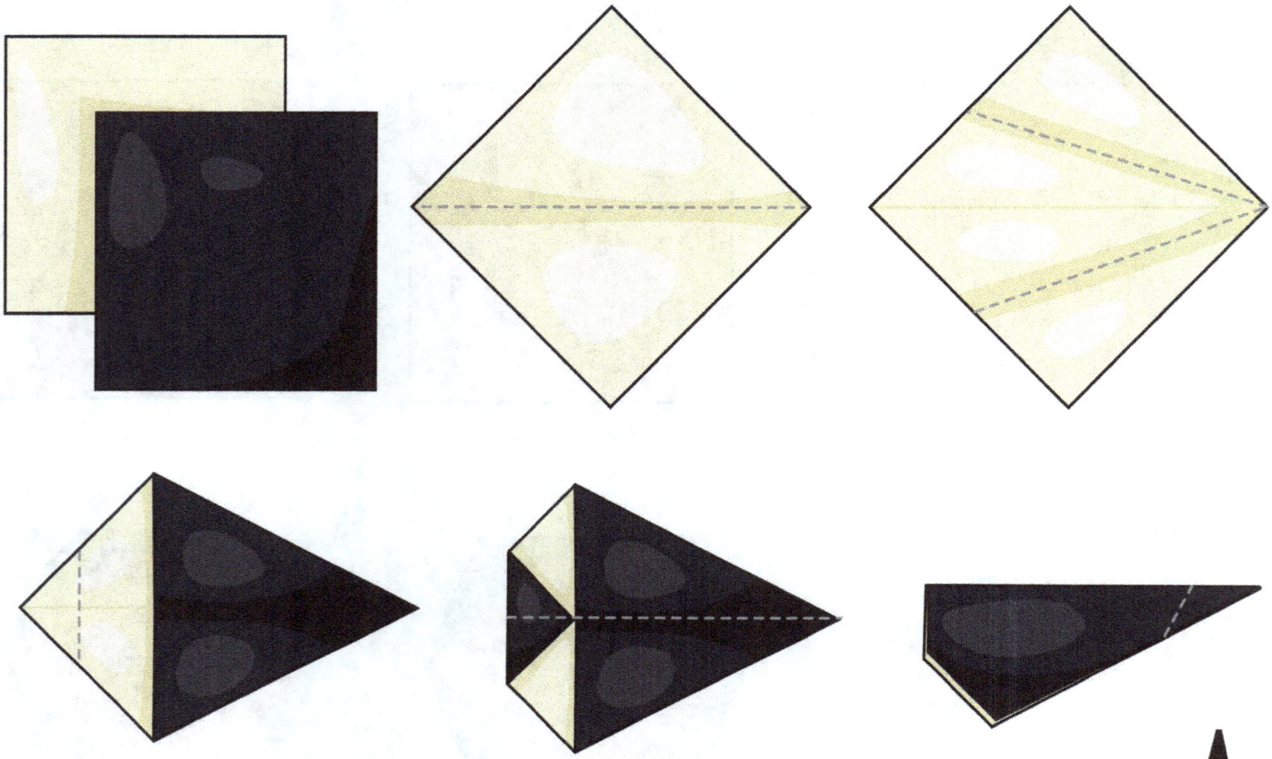

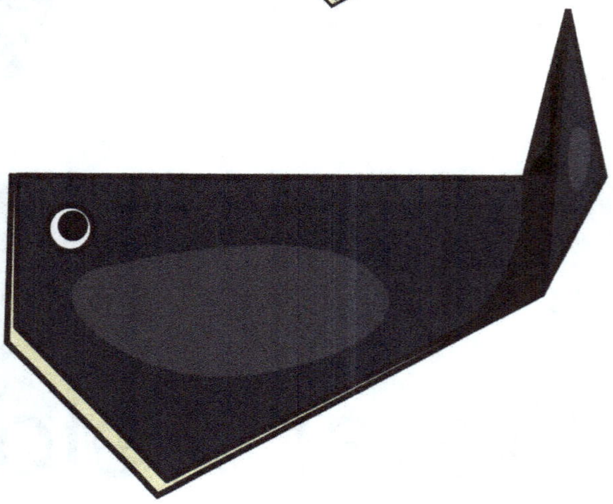

Whale

Balena

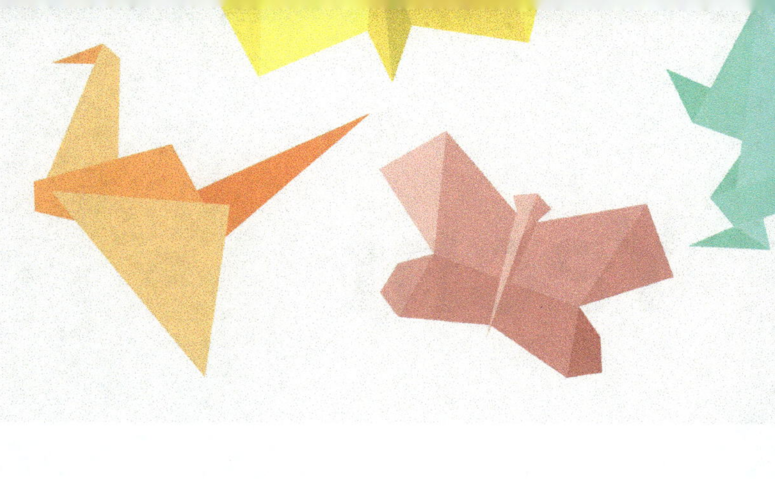

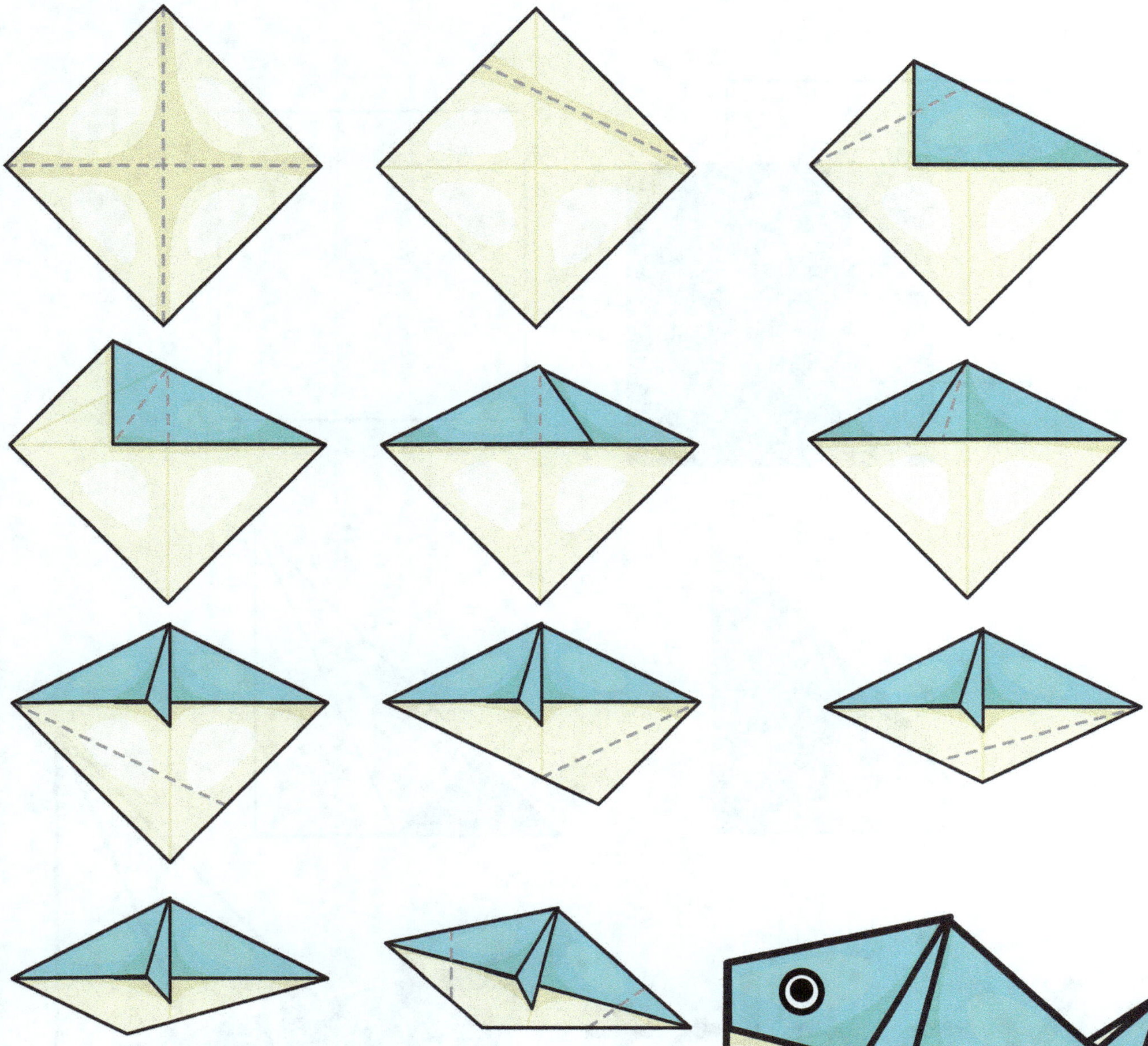

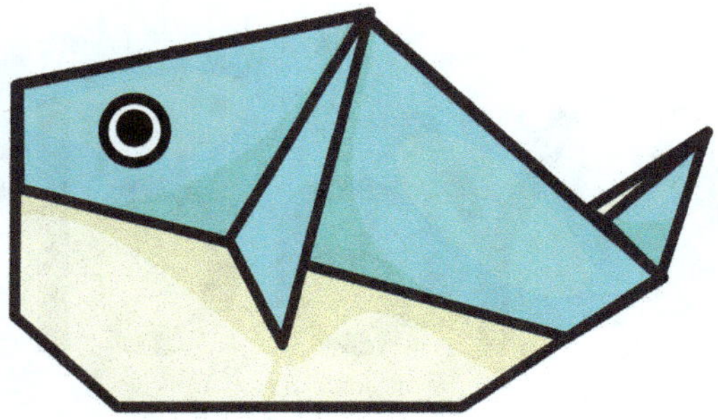

Whale 2

Yacht

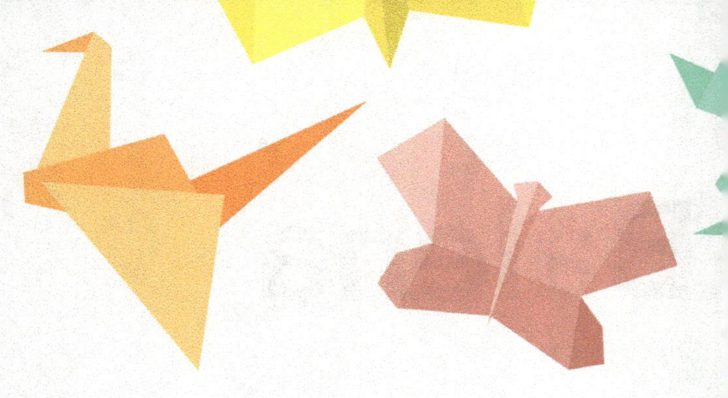

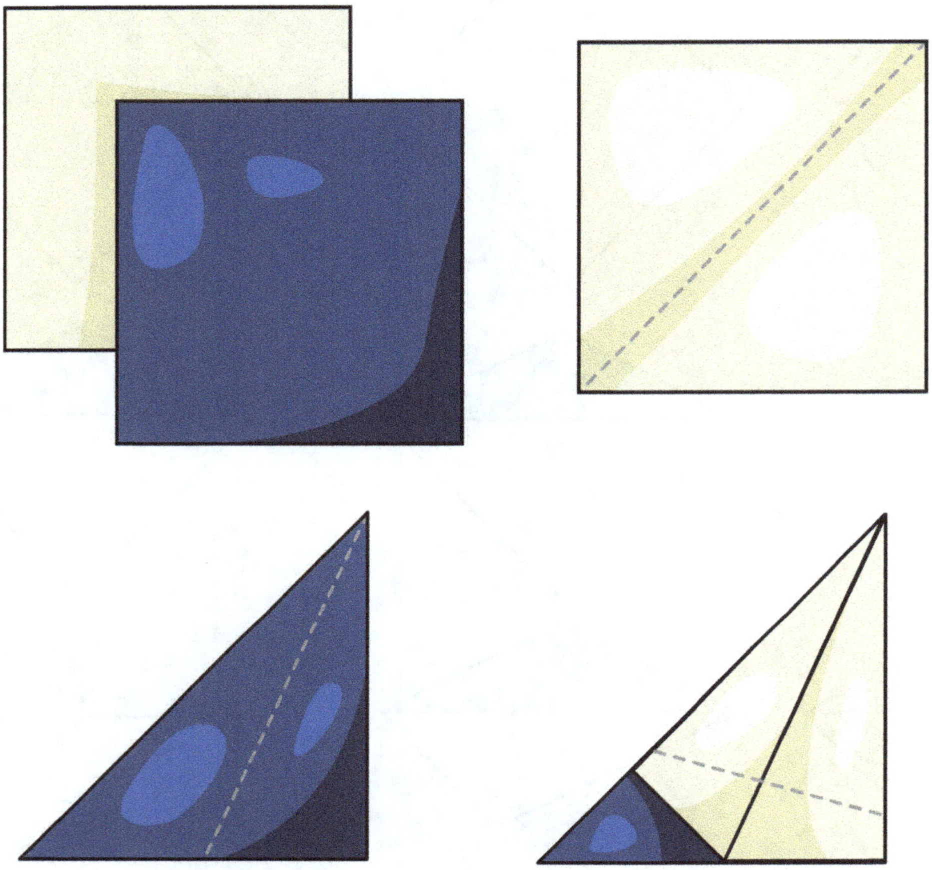

Yacht

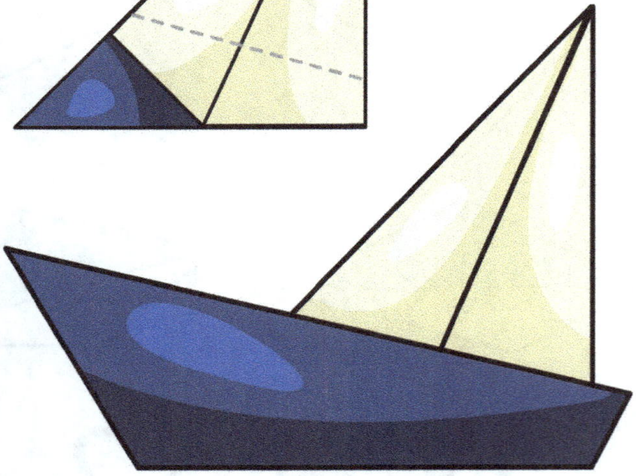

9 781635 895131